S
930
C 3
1967

CHARLES H. CALLISON is Executive Vice-President, National Audubon Society, New York. He has served as a member of the Federal Water Pollution Control Advisory Board, and is a former Chairman of the Natural Resources Council of America.

Other Books Sponsored by the
Natural Resources Council of America

Origins of American Conservation
HENRY CLEPPER, *Editor*

Careers in Conservation
HENRY CLEPPER, *Editor*

AMERICA'S NATURAL RESOURCES

Edited for the Natural Resources
Council of America

by

CHARLES H. CALLISON
NATIONAL AUDUBON SOCIETY

Revised Printing

THE RONALD PRESS COMPANY • NEW YORK

Copyright © 1967 by
THE RONALD PRESS COMPANY

Copyright © 1957 by
THE RONALD PRESS COMPANY

VR—VR

Library of Congress Catalog Card Number: 67–14482

PRINTED IN THE UNITED STATES OF AMERICA

PREFACE

More and more Americans are developing an appreciation for, and a conscience about, the natural resources of their continent. They are beginning to realize that nature's bounties are not inexhaustible, that careful husbanding is required if these resources are to continue to supply the needs of a complex civilization. The ideals of conservation are reflected in much legislation considered by Congress and state legislatures. Daily newspapers devote much space to resource management. Editors of popular magazines are paying increasing attention to the subject, and it has become a major issue in political campaigns.

Yet the vast majority of responsible citizens, however well meaning they may be, lack the essential background for an informed approach to the problems of conservation. It is to meet the need of such people that this book has been written. In the words of the nation's foremost experts, it brings together in brief, easily understandable form the basic facts on each of our major natural resources —soils, water, grasslands, forests, wildlife, fish, parks, and wilderness—showing where the principal dangers lie, what has been done to meet them, and what still urgently needs to be done. A separate chapter is devoted to each resource, so that the interested reader can quickly find what he needs to know about the question that immediately concerns him. But it is important to remember that all resources must be considered in relation to one another and managed as a whole. The introductory and final chapters are designed to make clear the broader picture, and each contributor has been at pains to point out the necessary interrelationships.

It is our hope that the book will be useful to readers in many situations. It may help voters make up their minds which of a pair of competing political candidates is talking sense about conservation. It may give practical information for farmers invited to help organize a watershed project, or teachers seeking sound concepts to present in their classes. It may provide guidance for legislators called on to vote on a controversial river basin bill, or editors who have to interpret the legislation. But above all, we shall be satisfied if the book brings home to the individual citizen the importance of conservation and the part he himself can play in his own community toward the promotion of sound practices.

The book is sponsored by the Natural Resources Council of America, a nonprofit, nonpolitical organization of thirty national and regional associations interested in the conservation and wise use of our renewable natural resources. The contributors were selected not only for their professional standing in their fields of specialization but also for their known objectivity. The goal of all has been to advance the attainment of sound management of natural resources in the public interest.

It is a pleasure to acknowledge the assistance given to this project by my colleagues on the Editorial Committee: Henry Clepper of the Society of American Foresters, who conceived the idea of this book; Michael Hudoba of the Outdoor Writers Association of America, and Richard W. Westwood of the American Nature Association.

Charles H. Callison
Chairman of the Editorial Committee

February, 1957

PREFACE
TO THE REVISED PRINTING

Although no longer a member of the Council's Editorial Committee, I have felt it a privilege to be charged with the editorial responsibility for this REVISED PRINTING. The book has been brought up to date with current statistics and in the light of recent legislation and includes discussions of the new Program for American Forestry and the Wilderness Act of 1964. My thanks go to the members of the Editorial Committee for their cooperation and support: Henry Clepper, Chairman; Daniel A. Poole of the Wildlife Management Institute; and the late Edward H. Graham.

Charles H. Callison

January, 1967

CONTENTS

AMERICA'S
NATURAL
RESOURCES

CHAPTER ONE

CONSERVATION: AN ECOLOGICAL APPROACH

Shirley W. Allen

Man's survival and his struggle for greater comfort and well-being are possible only through use of natural resources. These constitute his environment. They may be captured for use directly from nature as in the daily work of the lumberman, the farmer, the trapper, the miner, or the engineer, or employed indirectly as men use them after they have been captured, transported, processed, and marketed. In either instance men live off the natural resources. Men also enjoy the services of natural resources without drawing on them materially. Energy produced by harnessing falling water is an example of this. Enjoyment of the natural scene, moreover, helps men to build up their spiritual powers. How mankind manages natural resources, therefore, becomes of first importance. The modern automobile, for example, can hardly be produced without drawing in some measure on all classes of natural resources. It is by no means a

3

wholly mineral contraption, and its manufacture draws heavily on the plant world.

This dependence of man on resources is analogous to the related situation in nature where the natural resources utilize each other in their development. The duck which the hunter brings home would not have been available for his sport, and maybe would not be a duck at all, if any one of these things had been missing: water to drink and to rest on; vegetation for food, cover, and nest material; mineral matter in diet, at least enough to produce the shell of an egg; insects and other animal forms for food; the soil from which food and cover grow; the gravel to help digestion; and finally, the atmosphere through which to travel. It is not so easy to trace the contribution of the duck to the natural resources upon which he draws, but it can be done, if only in terms of droppings for fertilizer and seed distribution and of giving hitch-hiking insects a ride.

Let us take a tree, or a whole forest. Where does it fit into the picture as a user of other natural resources or a contributor to them? Well, it could not be a tree unless it could grow. It must have soil, water, air, and sunlight to grow. It draws, therefore, on minerals, water, and organic materials which other plants and certain animals have furnished to the soil. These latter become available through the action of water and microorganisms in the soil. In turn, the tree sheds its leaves and twigs to furnish some of this organic material or, if unharvested, falls eventually as red dust into the soil. Its crown breaks the tremendous beating power of rain drops on the soil. Its shade delays the melting of winter snows. Its accumulation of leaf- and twig-fall and the intricate pattern of roots help to gather rains which otherwise might be destructive runoff. Its branches and hollows furnish homes for various animals. It tempers the destructive force of winds. Its form and color and shade afford rest and inspiration to men, whose energy and powers are simply other kinds of natural resources.

And so one might go on selecting examples from each group of natural resources and pointing out the all-for-one and one-for-all relationships. But let it also be said that when man found himself in the Garden of Eden, he evidently decided on the spot that he was more than just an addition to the environment. Straightway he started using natural resources, and at the present writing his enthusiasm for this activity knows no bounds. Sometimes his tipping of nature's delicate balance becomes serious.

A Balance in Nature

To maintain some sort of a balance in nature in the face of the increasing numbers of men who have desires as well as needs is the business of conservation. The job splits three ways. First, there must be use of natural resources with minimum waste; second, they must be so used and managed that their productivity in terms of services and materials of quality shall be maintained and increased; and third, there must be equitable distribution of the products and services from natural resources, as among the present inhabitants of the earth and those who are to come. Achieving any one of these three objectives requires not only constant and vigorous physical effort, but also wisdom and understanding. Accomplishment of the first two—rational use, and maintenance of the power to produce (usually spoken of as productivity)—involves thorough and detailed understanding of the interrelationships of the natural resources themselves and of how much interference by man, with his mass-production economy, they will stand. To reach the third objective—fair distribution—requires up-to-date understanding of the needs men must fulfill to survive and of their wants over and above need. Certainly survival alone is not what we aim at in this country, and one is thought almost subversive if he suggests that our standard of living should ever begin to level off. Reward for service as against adjustment to need is a frequent conflict which society in general does not yet understand.

Because the conservation of natural resources is a complex business, the everyday citizen is likely to assume that he can do nothing about it. How it is brought about, therefore, is something on which he has a right to be informed. Then he will perhaps be more cautious about dismissing the subject with the remark, "There ought to be a law." And yet laws are important and necessary. They are the instruments by which much of our national and state policy is recorded and given authority. But the enacting and enforcing of laws is only one of many ways in which conservation is brought about. After all, the effectiveness of all conservation effort hangs largely on the attitude of the everyday citizen.

Understanding Natural Resources

Since information and understanding are necessary to assure correct attitudes, this book is designed to inform, and to bring about understanding of natural resources and their problems. The fact that the book has been prepared by a dozen authors, each writing within his own particular field, makes the total problem no less an attempt to reconcile the knowledge and the treatment of all natural resources—to emphasize the inescapable interdependence of resources, use, men, and action to conserve.

Careful and thoughtful reading will bring shock through apparent contradiction of commonly held opinions and beliefs. More than one city dweller, and even an occasional farmer, will be surprised to learn that soil is more than dirt, that it is teeming with life in the form of microorganisms. The businessman who takes a daily shower will read that water consumption in this country quadrupled between 1900 and 1950, and that by 1975, the 1950 figure is expected to double. It may even occur to him that he will have to use the same water over and over after it has been treated. The rancher, the woolgrower, and the western county supervisor will be likely to disagree with the idea that stock-raising is not the only beneficial use of grasslands and other forage-covered areas, but will be reminded that carrying capacity of the range must be respected. The man who is building his first house, and possibly the lumberman with whom he trades, will find out that the key to the nation's future timber supply lies with the millions of farm and other private holdings of forest land, 85 per cent of which are less than 100 acres in extent.

The ardent sportsman will be told that most of the "vermin"—predatory animals that he dislikes—are important if he is to continue to have exciting quarry to pursue. The fisherman who makes his living or gets his favorite recreation from catching fish may note that his license in the future will cost him more and the limit on catch become more restricted. The lover of solitude, or the person who thinks he loves solitude, will say "Amen" to the hint that wilderness is an irreplaceable natural resource. The park traveler will find recorded what he has long suspected, that national parks are not just samples of American landscape.

The crowded resident, the builder of a "thruway" which has long tangents and few curves, the subdivider, and the city council trying to locate a public dump will be asked to look twice before deciding that cornfields, park areas, and wild animal sanctuaries no longer need the space they occupy. The manufacturer or the metalworker will look in vain for a chapter on the energy and mineral resources, but they should be told that there is something wrong in the picture of a mad race to use up more and more of our irreplaceable minerals, leaving a trail of gutted countryside. Some worker, as he leaves home in the morning for his job, may rub his eyes, smarting from a smog-laden atmosphere, and wonder why that book had nothing to say about managing our fresh air resource. Finally, the good citizen who is already interested in conserving natural resources, and who wonders why its advocates cannot get together, will find some of the fundamentals of a national conservation policy about which he may never have thought.

Although the specialists who wrote the chapters that follow did not compare notes, the reader will note a similarity in conclusions that the tendency to waste, to accept a decline in productivity, and to play favorites among the users of natural resources must be overcome, even though such a course may go counter to modern technological thinking; that the foundation idea in conserving natural resources is the unity of nature; and that our job is not so much conquering natural forces, as it is cooperating with nature, of which we ourselves are a part.

For Further Reading

ALLEN, SHIRLEY W., and JUSTIN W. LEONARD. 1966. *Conserving Natural Resources—Principles and Practice in a Democracy.* McGraw-Hill Book Co., New York. 3d ed. 432 pp.

American Forests—The Magazine of Forests, Soil, Water, Wildlife, and Outdoor Recreation. Monthly. The American Forestry Association, Washington, D.C.

TRAIN, RUSSELL E. 1965. *America the Beautiful.* Address before the 90th annual meeting of The American Forestry Association at Jackson Lake, Grand Teton National Park, Wyoming, September 6, 1965. The Conservation Foundation, New York.

UDALL, STEWART L. 1963. *The Quiet Crisis.* Holt, Rinehart & Winston, Inc., New York. 209 pp.

CHAPTER TWO

RENEWABLE RESOURCES AND HUMAN POPULATIONS

Fairfield Osborn

About six thousand years ago, communities of men probably faced their first problem resulting from increasing population and shortage of food supply and other resources. Such a crisis may have occurred in a region in China, in a hidden valley in Asia Minor, or in the land of the early Egyptians. Shortage of raw materials is an old story, as is starvation, the menacing specter. The point is that through thousands of years of time, mankind has had to struggle to get a living from the earth.

It seems well to approach today's worldwide problem of renewable resources and human populations with some such historical perspective as the above. We are dealing with an age-old question. Yet it is one that in this twentieth century is untellably more complex, and one in which all people everywhere are profoundly involved. The question of the adequacy of natural resources for a rapidly growing world population that has increased so fantastically within the last two centuries has now become "everybody's business."

We Americans, because of the extraordinary richness of our own natural resources, are inclined to commiserate with countries such as India, Japan, and China, or with certain countries in Latin America and even Europe, and say to ourselves: "It's too bad that this country or that is facing such a problem—we can be grateful that it isn't ours." In doing this, we may be overlooking the fact that we ourselves are even now entering a phase in our national life in which our basic natural resources may not prove adequate for our rapidly increasing population and spiraling industrial demands.

Worldwide Conditions

Let us first look at the world picture, going back a little in time in order to get a wider vision of what has been taking place. Three hundred years ago, in the middle of the seventeenth century, the world's population is estimated to have been approximately 470 million people, or about one-seventh of today's number. There are various valid reasons for assuming that it had not previously exceeded that figure. However, the eighteenth century proved to be a period of major change. It witnessed the beginnings of better means of communication and transport, the introduction of the steam engine, and the beginning of improvements in medical care. It was a time of stirring, of new impulses, of final breaking away from the prolonged era of medievalism. The revelation of the great wealth of the Western Hemisphere had a profound psychological effect upon the minds of men. The fascination of new horizons galvanized the thoughts of European peoples. In a material sense, this New World soon began to contribute to the welfare of Europe. Soon the Far East began to share these new influences. In effect the eighteenth century was a growing period—the dawn of the industrial revolution. As a consequence of these various encouraging developments, the population of the world increased by about 400 million people in a century and a half, and at the opening of the nineteenth century had risen to about 870 million people.

Then there came, at a steady accelerating rate, the explosive increase in human numbers. The new forces of industrial production, the extension of commerce, rapid transport of food and other materials, and, above all, the revolutionary advances in the medical sciences spread their influences throughout the world. From the point of view of population growth, the most important factor was the widespread adoption of better sanitation, the control of pestilence and plagues, and the consequent lowering of the death rate, including infant mortality. These advances, in greater or less degree, affected every country, whether in Europe, the New World, or the Orient. In the short span of four generations, or one hundred years, the world's population almost doubled, and as the twentieth century opened, it stood at approximately 1.6 billion people.

Since 1900 this extraordinary upward surge in the numbers of people has continued. Another 1.7 billion have been added to the world population within the past 65 years, bringing the figure in 1965 up to about 3.3 billion. By the end of this century, *if present rates of increase continue,* and barring a cataclysm such as atomic war, the total world population should exceed 7 billion.

There are various ways by which one can attempt to

visualize the significance of this almost incredible population growth. For instance, the present rate of increase results, each year, in approximately 69.3 million additional people—a number almost equal to the population of eight cities the size of London or New York or Toyko. Perhaps a more vivid comparison is that the increase since the year 1900, namely, some 1.7 billion people, doubles the sum total of the populations of Europe, North and South America, and Africa in that year. No wonder we are witness to a succession of violent and mounting pressures upon the social and political institutions of our times.

The whole question as to whether the earth can continue to support such rapidly increasing populations is, as is to be expected, a subject of wide and growing controversy, spearheaded by two divergent schools of thought. One school rests its case on the resilient capacity of technology to discover new sources of raw materials, or substitutes for vanishing raw materials, and even envisages that science can somehow produce entirely new sources of food supply. The other school takes the position that today and tomorrow, as throughout all history, mankind will continue to be primarily dependent upon the productive capacity of the earth, especially as far as *renewable resources* are concerned.

The argument between the two current schools of thought will undoubtedly continue. At this time there is indeed ample justification for marveling at the accomplishments of the technical sciences. Through them we have gained an infinitely clearer understanding of the physical world in which we live, even of the universe of which our small planet is only a minute fraction. Through science, too, new sources of energy are being developed, new reserves of raw materials are being exploited, new methods of obtaining water supply or food substitutes are being explored, and new and improved agricultural techniques are being adopted. No one can predict what new revelations and discoveries lie ahead.

Nevertheless, in the midst of this "Atomic Age" the people of the earth must still rely on the primary elements of the earth, such as fresh water supply, vegetation in all its forms from crops to forests, and the infinite varieties of animal life, seen and unseen, that contribute to the vitality of the "living earth."

There is another aspect of the question of renewable resources that is often overlooked. At the present time, the greater part of human society is economically and culturally engaged in agricultural pursuits. It is true that in an industrial country such as the United States, the number of people so engaged is relatively small compared to the total population—far smaller than in most of the countries of the world. But the fact remains that agriculture is "the way of life" of the greater part of the world's people.

In a highly industrialized country it is a temptation to assume that "industrialization" will prove a ready panacea for people in other lands, especially those that we in the Western world frequently refer to as "underdeveloped." However, industrialization is only one avenue to the improvement of human welfare, and great damage can be done to agricultural societies if its adoption is too greatly hastened or overemphasized. Aside from the challenge to technology to find new sources of raw materials or to provide substitutes for those natural resources that are now becoming scarce, there is great need for improvement in the handling of *renewable* resources, as regards both water-supply and agricultural techniques in general. One can sense that, as time runs on, the purposes of the presently conflicting schools of thought will draw ever closer together. One fundamental premise can presumably be accepted by both, namely, that renewable resources will continue to prove vital to the welfare of man as far as one dares to look ahead into the future. The need on the national scene as well as on the world scene is to devise the most effective methods of developing and using these resources.

At present, the world is not keeping pace with the growing requirements of rapidly increasing populations, even in the primary category of food supply. During several recent years the reports by the Food and Agriculture Organization of the United Nations have reflected this. The next forty or fifty years will certainly produce a series of crises the dimensions of which cannot yet be estimated. By the end of the century, as noted above, there is the actual possibility that the world's population may have increased by another three to four billion people. At this moment hundreds of millions of people are at a level of want, if not of near-starvation. One thing is clear: the need of adequate renewable resources is constantly becoming more imperative.

In considering the whole subject of ever increasing numbers of human beings and the problem of providing for their welfare, we find that an insistent question is now thrusting itself into the minds of people and even into the plans of governments. There is a new consciousness that the sole desideratum is not *quantity* as regards either human numbers or resources. Must not the *quality* of life that human society is capable of creating for its own future also be considered? This awareness has not come voluntarily, so to speak, but through the force of present pressures and the realization that these pressures will increase rather than subside. As a consequence, there is growing recognition that active and earnest thought must be given to controlling population growth. It is now recognized throughout the world that a rational control of human reproduction is, in many respects, the most important problem that faces mankind. We live in a period when, for compelling reasons, peace between nations is being sought as never before. We are becoming conscious of the fact that there can be no peace if the present pressures of growing populations and diminishing resources continue indefinitely.

What of the position of the United States in regard to both populations and renewable resources? Before touching upon our domestic situation, we might initially consider to what degree our country could contribute toward resolving the world population problem in either of two ways: first, by providing food for people living in great want in other parts of the world; second, by openly and vigorously endorsing the need of birth control and developing practical methods to accomplish it both at home and abroad.

The Problem of Food

The export of our country's surplus grains and other food supplies to other countries faced with famine is at best a stopgap and emergency measure. It is a gesture of humanitarianism that we have every reason to make, falling, as it does, within our overall foreign program of helping people in other parts of the world who are less fortunate than ourselves. But as a long-term cure for meeting world food shortages it is virtually meaningless.

Our supplying wheat to India, for instance, whose food shortages always represent an acute problem, cannot really meet its needs. Even now the most recent estimates indicate that our reserve of wheat stocks represents merely one year's supply and could fall considerably lower during the years immediately ahead. Only five years ago our reserve was five times as great. Thus it is highly improbable that the United States, in the face of increasing demands from its own rapidly growing population, will continue to have wheat surpluses as large as those of recent years.

Another facet is that the people of India are, to a large degree, habituated to a diet of rice and much prefer not to adjust their diets to other grains.

Immigration and Population

Some years ago, when the world's "population explosion" began to work itself keenly into public consciousness, there was considerable attention given to the idea that the United States could help to relieve the situation by receiving a far greater number of immigrants from other countries. In the earlier history of our country this movement of peoples was advantageous; in fact, without it, the United States could never have attained its present position. America's greatness is derived to a considerable degree by the successful amalgamation of foreign peoples, heretofore unparalleled elsewhere in the history of any other nation. But even now, even so soon, there is no more "room." Our cities cannot absorb more, our agricultural lands do not require more, our great industrial complex does not require more, our own population is increasing too rapidly as it is. The sign along the highways—*No Vacancy*—has become the symbol of reality. Fortunately, the rate of our national population growth is now beginning somewhat to decline. One can only hope that this trend will continue through many years ahead.

Thus, the only solution to this world problem lies in a step-up of food production together with limitation of population growth, region by region and country by country. Consequently, much as the United States may wish to help, its best contribution would appear to be the continuance and even expansion of its technical assistance programs, either directly or through the United Nations, to less developed and needier countries. *The great hope lies in each country's developing its own resources and facing its own population problem.*

America's Situation

Now, what of the situation of our country as regards its population and its renewable resources? As to the former, we are only beginning to become aware of the implications of our own rapid national population growth.

Estimates as to our future population naturally vary considerably. Some prognostications indicate that we may have considerably more than 300 million people in this country by the end of the century. The forecasters of population growth are as subject to error as those of the weather. However, it seems highly probable that we shall have a considerably larger population within the next generation. Already every region and community in our country is beginning to sense the consequences of these growing pressures. Perhaps we are becoming aware of them because of housing shortages, or through the inconveniences resulting from traffic congestion, or through the evident difficulties our educational system faces in properly meeting the needs of an ever larger number of students. These are, in effect, *social* problems, which in one way or another will have to be solved—although how satisfactorily is another matter. One wonders when the time will come in which the people of our country may ask, "What, after all, is an optimum population for this nation of ours?" In asking this primary question, although we are not yet prepared to deal with it, we can take an important step toward becoming masters of our own destiny.

Underneath such *social* problems lie the essential *physical* needs of our people, which must be met from our own natural resources or those imported from other lands. Throughout most of our nation's history we were virtually self-sufficient so far as natural resources were concerned. This is no longer true. For example, in 1900 we produced some 15 per cent more raw materials than we consumed, exclusive of food. Today we are consuming far more materials than we are producing—even as much as one-fifth more.

The future size of our population has, of course, a tremendous bearing upon the adequacy of our renewable resources. Many of the answers to questions concerning our nation's position with respect to these resources will be found in other chapters of this book dealing with soils, water, grasslands, forests, wildlife, and marine life. All are vital to our economy as well as to our culture. To illustrate the interrelated values of any one resource to all the others, a few comments may be made here concerning water resources, which in many respects is the key resource of them all.

It is too easy to overlook the fact that our unparalleled

position of wealth, whether derived from agriculture or from industry, would have been impossible if our continent were not so richly endowed with water. Compare, for example, our position with that of Australia, a country whose size is virtually identical with ours, yet which presently supports a population equivalent only to a little over 11 million. The small population of Australia is not due solely to lack of water. Yet it is estimated that the largest population that Australia could support is between 40 and 50 million people, a number rigidly controlled by its existing water resources.

There are striking contrasts in our country—from East to West and from the Pacific Northwest to the arid Southwest—of regions rich in water and of regions relatively poor or altogether lacking. Within each of these regions there are, in turn, great diversities in local water environments and, hence, in water problems. Obviously, many factors enter into the availability and control of water in any one place. Climate, geology, soils, and vegetation are some of the evident natural or physical factors; population density, land use, industrialization, engineering structures such as dams and levees, and pollution are some of the factors related to human use—or misuse. Nor can we overlook political and cultural factors. It was no accident, for instance, that the Mormons developed such an efficient irrigation agriculture in Utah.

The rapid increase in the use of water is an interesting phenomenon of the modern age. Gone are the primitive homestead days when two buckets for each person would do. Vast cities, industrial systems, irrigated lands have changed all that. Today our per capita withdrawals of water are approximately 1,800 gallons per day, a figure almost four times that of the year 1900. Our population has also more than doubled since 1900, so that our total national use has increased almost seven times in the past sixty-five years. Less than half of this withdrawn water is actually used up; at least 60 per cent of the water withdrawn by municipalities is returned to some water source; about 90 per cent of the industrial withdrawal is returned, as is some 30 per cent of the water used for irrigation. However—and this is an important point—most of this used water is returned polluted by wastes that either prevent or severely limit its reuse.

With the great growth of industry, and with the continuing growth of urban areas and the spread of irrigation in the East as well as the West, the nation has been made more aware of the "water problem." A lot of thinking has been done on many aspects of water resources. Over recent years we have benefited from the work of the Hoover Commission, the President's Water Policy Commission, the President's Materials Policy Commission, and latterly, the Federal Water Pollution Control Administration. The work of these bodies, and of the many professional and other groups that contributed their findings and views, has clarified many questions that are involved so that we can now see issues and alternatives. Of course, much remains inescapably controversial, such as the question of public vs. private power development, and the role of the federal government in resource development. One fact, however, stands out in the findings of those who have examined our national water problems. It is not in the least controversial. It is that we *know* far too little about the many varying conditions determining the quantity of water that is naturally available.

We cannot afford to underestimate the serious implications of our national water problem. Already approximately one-quarter of our total population, some 50 million citizens in various parts of the country, are in real trouble because of inadequate supply or unsatisfactory quality. The combined factors of an increasing population and steadily mounting demands are making the situation more acute as each year passes. Unless we put far more thought and energy into resolving the problem, we shall become involved in difficulties that can shackle much of our economy and jeopardize the welfare of a large proportion of our people.

The Conservation Movement

Undoubtedly the most promising influence upon the future status of our nation's renewable resources is the growth of what, for lack of a better term, can be called the "conservation movement." The last two decades have witnessed a remarkable increase in interest on the part of government, industry, and public alike. This awakening has led to improvement in forest practices, advancement in agricultural techniques, greater study of the water problem, and wider recognition that wildlife and natural areas must be protected.

The greater part of this chapter has been devoted to the consideration of purely physical resources. But we must also realize that one of the most essential needs of our times is to preserve the heritage of nature. Too few people concede that man, in gaining mastery over the physical world, threatens to leave behind him waste and desolation for generations still unborn. Too few people acknowledge that we of this hurrying, driving, materialistic age still must be trustees of the past for the good of the future. Surely we must be profoundly aware of the fact that the wonders of the natural world, once destroyed, can never be replaced. The soul of a people can wither unless refreshed by nature. Consequently, while assuring the long-term availability of our natural resources for material use, we also must protect, or rather, improve the natural environment in which the people of our country live. We must preserve sufficient wilderness areas, protect our wildlife, and sustain such invaluable assets as our national parks and other recreation areas.

The future of our natural resources is secure if we make it so. It remains to be demonstrated, however, whether we as a nation are prepared to exercise all of the foresight and all of the skills, and even make some of the sacrifices, that will be required if our renewable resources are to meet the increasing pressures upon them from our expanding industrial system and our growing population.

CHAPTER THREE

SOIL

Firman E. Bear and Selden Lee Tinsley

The total land area of our fifty United States is 2,298 million acres. Of this, about 633 million acres are range or pastureland that is too dry or too rough for growing harvested crops. Some 773 million acres are covered with forest or woodland, and 277 million acres are desert, mountain, swamp, or waste. Our cities, homesteads, roads, railroads, and the like occupy another 157 million acres. This leaves 458 million acres now in use for crop production. The U.S. Department of Agriculture estimates that 75 million acres of land presently used for cultivated crops is better suited for pasture or forest while 250 million acres in these less intensive uses is suitable for crop production. Thus, there are about 633 million acres of land that could be used for cropland if needed.

The soil that covers the major part of this vast land area varies greatly from region to region. This variation resulted primarily from the kind of rock from which the soil was formed and on the nature of the associated climate and vegetation. Soil, climate, and vegetation are so interrelated that if one has detailed information about any one of these three, he has a fairly dependable basis for judging the nature of the other two.

Soil is an intimate mixture of small particles of rock residues with decaying vegetable matter. It forms a workable layer of great variety of color, composition, and depth underlying the present vegetative cover and overlying the rocks that constitute the earth's solid crust. Within every pound of it many billions of microbes are digesting the refuse of previous plants and releasing the nutrient elements that they contain for reuse by plants. And they are also acting on the soil minerals to release additional nutrients for crop use.

The sun shines on the soil. The air sweeps over it. The rain falls on it. Warmth, air, and water move upward and downward through it. The soil's microbial population flourishes or fades depending on the management the soil receives at the hands of man. Soil, therefore, is not a dead, unchangeable product but a living dynamic thing with potentialities for marked improvement in its crop-producing capacity. But it can readily be ruined by careless handling. Often it is ruined beyond repair.

Climate tends to be the dominant factor in soil formation. In fact, it is so much so that most mature soils in a given climatic zone tend to have essentially the same composition no matter what the nature of the rock from which they were derived. This applies to soils having their origin in such widely diverse rocks as limestone, shale, and granite. Young soils, like those found on steep slopes, tend toward much closer chemical relationship to the original rocks than mature soils.

Since natural vegetation can be more readily classified than either the climatic complex or the soil, the first maps of our land resources outlined the areas of tree, grass, and desert growth. Such maps showed forest cover over virtually all the land east of the Mississippi River and from St. Louis into southwestern Texas. To the west of the forest area were, successively, the tall-grass prairies —which extended east of the Mississippi River into northern Illinois; the short-grass treeless plains; and the mesquite, sagebrush, and cactus in still drier areas farther westward. In the far Northwest, trees were again encountered, as they were also in the mountains of the drier regions.

At present we are harvesting cultivated crops or tame hay from 458 million acres. By drainage of swamp land, bringing more desert land under irrigation, and converting some of the better pasture and woodland to cultivation, we could increase our cultivated cropland to well over 600 million acres. This acreage, when considered with an ever improving agricultural technology, is sufficient to feed any presently envisioned population. It might even be extended by reclaiming some of the shallow areas along our shores. Any such conversion of shallow shoreland or inland wetlands would result in corresponding decreases in fishery resources and wildlife that are naturally dependent upon such habitat.

The remaining 1,698 million acres include not only the needed reserves for grazing and forestry, but also vast expanses of desert and widely scattered areas that are of primary value for recreational purposes and for game and fish preserves. The people who live in the more densely populated parts of our country need to be constantly alert to the necessity of protecting these recreational areas against encroachment by industry and agriculture. Similarly, agriculture must be on guard that industry, transportation, and cities do not encroach unduly on the better farming land of our country. Good farm land lost to urbanization moves agriculture to less suitable areas and results in higher priced food for everyone.

Destructive Soil Erosion

For thousands of years before the Americas were discovered by Columbus, most of the soil of this continent was sewed to the Earth by the roots of trees and grass. But no sooner had the pioneers arrived than they set to work cutting down the forest and tearing up the sod. Soon the soil started downhill. Only a little over three centuries had elapsed before our attention was forcibly directed to the destructive effects of wind and water, which were rapidly eroding the soil away. Hurried investigation of this problem soon revealed that far too much of our rich virgin topsoil had already disappeared and that, over increasingly large areas, we were now farming the much less productive subsoil. In many locations erosion had eaten down to the useless rocks beneath.

The farmers of the United States have dug their way down into the subsoil faster than those of any other nation that ever existed. In part, this was because we had large expanses of land; in part, the pattern of rainfall can be blamed. But it was due even more to the corn, potatoes, tobacco, and tomatoes that we inherited from the Indians and to the cotton that thrived in the South. The peculiar thing about all these crops was that the land had to be plowed in preparation for growing them and that cultivation was required between the rows.

Being a nation of ingenious people, we soon developed bigger and better plows, and tractors to pull them. And, for many years, advertisements showing these plows and tractors at work pictured long straight furrows, no matter where they were leading. The slightest crook eliminated the contestant in the highly popular plowing tournaments.

But not all of our troubles are due to the plow and the

clean-cultivated crops that tend to follow its use. This is a land of heavy downpours, and often of long periods of drought in between. Most of our European ancestors were accustomed to farming under conditions of frequent light showers. The average annual rainfall in the vicinity of London, Paris, and Berlin is of the order of 25 to 30 inches. Year-round green grass tells the story of the climate of those areas, whereas storms, floods, and dust bowls illustrate the climate in America.

Early in the history of the agriculture of this country, the heavy rains and strong winds presented some very troublesome problems. And these problems grew in number and in size as more and more of the land lost its native tree and grass cover. This was particularly noticeable in the southeastern part of the nation, where the land was rolling, the summers were long and hot, and the rainfall was heavy.

In this area soil erosion forced its attention on farmers. Yet relatively little was done about it until Hugh H. Bennett, the son of a North Carolina farmer, and a man who cared, came on the scene during the 1920's. As a soil survey specialist for the U.S. Department of Agriculture, Bennett had abundant opportunity to study the land at first hand. And he was worried about what he saw. Everywhere he went the handwriting of erosion was apparent in the ever deepening gullies. The streams ran red with soil after every rain. He expanded his studies to include the entire South, and Cuba and Puerto Rico as well. And he was even more convinced that national legislation was necessary if the soil of this country was to be adequately preserved for the use of future generations of farmers.

Bennett did not advocate eliminating the plow. Instead he and his associates suggested merely a change in direction for it—plowing along the contour of the land instead of in straight lines. This did away with the downhill channels that hastened the flow of water and a rapid and extensive loss of topsoil.

Bennett was particularly disturbed by land that was allowed to lie bare during the winter months, after a crop of corn or cotton had been harvested from it, for the rain beat directly on the soil in these bare fields, loosening the clay particles and carrying them off the field in quantity. What was needed was some system by which a permanent cover was maintained over the land, except for the short periods while it was being plowed and planted.

Under his leadership a great variety of methods was developed for protecting the land in the interim between one crop and the next. Cover crops were planted late in the season so that when the rain fell, it would strike the leaves of these plants and flow slowly down the stems instead of striking the soil directly. Row crops were rotated with close-growing crops to build erosion-resisting organic matter in the soil. Much more attention was given to seeding the rough land with permanent grass and to planting forest trees in the areas where crop production was not advisable.

The Soil Conservation Movement

Preliminary work on soil conservation was carried out under the auspices of the Soil Erosion Service, which was established in 1933. A great dust storm occurred on May 12, 1934, in western Kansas, Oklahoma, and Texas. The skies of the whole nation from there eastward were darkened by the dust. Residents of New York and Boston, and elsewhere throughout the East, were brought face to face with the facts of soil destruction. Many people realized for the first time that our luxurious food supplies, which they had long taken for granted, might soon be in danger.

Congress took immediate steps to establish a permanent Soil Conservation Service, which came into being with the passage of the Soil Conservation Act of 1935. Thus, the problem was recognized nationally, the Service was organized with Bennett at its head, and the necessary technical staff was assembled. Conservation education programs were quickly put into operation, the country over, on a state-by-state basis. This act is probably the most important piece of national legislation with respect to the conservation of land resources that the world has ever known. Its principles have been adopted by many other nations.

Yet more than this act was required to put conservation on the land. At first farmers stood on the sidelines, taking the measure of the Soil Conservation Service. The land they worked was theirs, having been won from Indians, forests, prairies, plains, and swamps. They were not inclined to look with favor on a federal agency that had come to tell them what to do with their own soil and how to do it.

Being intelligent men, they soon realized, however, that such an agency might well be of great help in fighting the forces that nature had arrayed against them. These forces are nowhere so apparent as out in the open country, on the hillsides of the East, and across the vast prairies and plains of the West. In due time, therefore, these farmers sat down with the conservationists to talk things over. Out of these talks came the concept of soil conservation districts, operating under state and local rather than federal control.

Experience with this type of joint enterprise quickly

convinced the more capable leaders that such a district provided a real opportunity for community accomplishment. The soil conservation districts became agencies that gradually covered the major part of the land area of the nation. Each district is supervised by from three to five farmers, who are in a position to render highly important services to their neighbors. In a way, these farmers are working for themselves. But they are also working for their communities and for the nation as a whole. They represent a highly enlightened type of selfishness for all the people, everywhere.

A district may be a valley, a watershed, a county, or several counties joined together. District supervisors have four primary functions: (1) to promote conservation among their neighbors; (2) to bring their communities together to consider the land problems they have in common; (3) to enlist the aid not only of the Soil Conservation Service technicians, but of all the other federal, state, county, and local agencies that can lend a hand; and (4) to govern their districts, not by compulsion, but by persuasion.

District supervisors initiate, supervise, and control, always keeping in mind the attitudes and desires of the local people. Sometimes group interest may be primarily in liming, drainage, land-leveling, terrace-building, pond-construction, contour planting, sodded waterways, or pasture-improvement. Whatever it is, this interest provides a starting point out of which an overall conservation program can be developed. Often progress is slow, but sometimes it is very rapid indeed.

An example of effective work on the part of a Soil Conservation District under the direction of capable supervisors is provided by a report from F. R. Hothem, a former district supervisor for Coshocton County, Ohio.

He writes: "In the late thirties one of our farmers saw contour strip cropping on a trip in the South. On his return he contacted our county agent, Harold Chambers, in regard to getting some strips established on his farm. Chambers secured the services of Ralph Bazler of the Soil Conservation Service and together they established three pilot or demonstration farms.

"A short time later a C.C.C. Camp, located at Mt. Vernon, Ohio, began work on a few farms by planting trees, removing fence rows, laying out strips, building contour fences, constructing diversions and establishing other conservation practices. About the same time the Soil Conservation Service set up a hydrologic research station in our county. This work was on a watershed basis and the above conservation practices were applied to farms in this watershed.

"Since contour farming was new and an entirely different way of farming, it was watched very closely by adjoining farmers. It didn't take long for some of them to see the benefits of saving soil and water and thereby getting increased yields. Each year more and more farmers came to the county agent for help in laying out strips until he could not keep up with the requests.

"In 1941, the state legislature passed the district-enabling act. The county agent immediately organized a sponsoring committee and the Coshocton Soil Conservation District, the second in Ohio, was organized in 1942.

"Because of the groundwork previously done, farmer interest was high. The main thing needed was technical assistance to help the farmer establish the conservation practices. After the organization of the District, this was supplied by the Soil Conservation Service through the District.

"By the creation of a District and the assignment of

regular technicians, the program soon evolved from one-practice, contour strip-cropping to one that covered the entire farm, including cropland, pasture, and woodland.

"Some of the accomplishments to date are: 920 district cooperators (60 per cent of operating units); 38,500 acres of contour strip-cropping; 13 miles of diversion terraces; 120 miles of tile and 20 miles of open ditch; 85 farm ponds built; 300 springs developed for livestock watering; 37,000 acres of pasture renovated; 41,000 acres in improved rotations; 3,900 acres reforested; 32,000 acres of woods protected from livestock; and 700 acres of wildlife land developed. Another very noticeable change is the increased use of lime and fertilizer. Significant changes have been effected in the use of cropland, more intensive rotations having been adopted on the level areas and more of the sloping land having been seeded to grass.

"Coshocton County, being in the Appalachian region, has an abundance of bituminous coal at shallow depth. Surface mining is increasing at a rapid rate. About 10,000 acres have already been strip mined. This has reduced the number of farming units. Much of this mined land, however, has been or soon will be converted to wildlife, forest and pasture uses.

"The District program is constantly changing to keep up with the desires of the people. Need for use of more land for recreation purposes is recognized and many wildlife and recreation units are being developed.

"The district supervisors have done a good job of conservation on their own farms and have shown outstanding leadership in guiding the conservation movement in the county. This leadership resulted in the winning of the Goodyear Conservation Award in the state one year and in being runner-up on several other occasions.

"Soil conservation in Coshocton County has been an

action program. The District Supervisors and the Soil Conservation Service personnel have worked closely in promoting soil and water conservation and have followed through to give prompt and efficient service to the cooperators in the District. The North Appalachia Soil and Water Experiment Station, located in the county, has contributed its full share to the teamwork required in getting the job done.

"The Soil Conservation Service has contributed a lot to agricultural development in this county. If a soil conservation program is to be applied to the farms, we must have technical assistance available to help the farmers establish these practices. We would never have gotten very far in our district without it."

This is democracy at work from the ground up. The district supervisors are elected by their neighbors or they are appointed by their state soil conservation committees. Their function is to protect their own communities against the ravages of wind and water and against misuse of land. And the people in these districts also look forward to a fuller realization of the potentialities of their land and water resources. They are building a better America out on the farms of this country, not for themselves alone but for all the people of this nation. They constitute our first line of defense against national decadence.

Watershed Programs

As farmers, district supervisors, and soil conservationists worked with the soil, it became increasingly clear that soil problems and water problems were inseparable. It also became apparent that many soil and water problems extended over farm boundaries and must be approached on a watershed basis. Thus, in 1954 Congress supplemented the Soil Conservation Act with the Watershed Protection and Flood Prevention Act.

Under this authorization the Soil Conservation Service assists districts, counties, and other local governments with the solution of watershed-wide soil and water problems. Structures for flood prevention, drainage, irrigation, fish and wildlife, and recreation may be included in a watershed project. Land treatment—tying down the soil with a mat of vegetation, contouring, and terracing—is a basic part of all watershed projects.

The recently authorized Assunpink watershed project adjacent to Trenton, New Jersey, is an excellent example. Flood problems had plagued the city of Trenton and adjacent Hamilton Township. Farmers in the upper reaches of the stream were bothered not only by flooding but also by poor drainage.

The state, two counties, three townships, two soil conservation districts, and the Soil Conservation Service joined together—under the leadership of the district supervisors—and developed a common solution to the problem. Salient features include eleven dams and twelve miles of channel improvement. All of the dams are designed to alleviate flooding. Eight of them will also be used for recreation. A 2000-acre county park, a 4700-acre state park, and a 300-acre township park are coming into being around these lakes. Two lakes will also be used to regulate the flow of the stream during dry periods. As in all watershed projects, landowners are cooperating with the soil conservation districts in accelerating land treatment to hold the soil in place and reduce siltation coming into the lakes.

Soil Surveys

Related to its activities with the soil conservation districts, the Soil Conservation Service gives leadership to the National Cooperative Soil Survey. This calls for the making of detailed maps that show not only the soil types, but also the slope of the land and the kind and degree of erosion now taking place, or potentially possible. This land-mapping program provides an opportunity to break up some of the more generalized soil types into smaller units that have important meaning to those who use the land.

The starting point in the soil survey is to establish the soil type. This includes both a *series* name, derived from the area in which a soil of the characteristics included was first mapped, and a word or words defining the percentages of sand, silt, and clay contained in it. Thus the type defines the color of the soil, its chemical reaction, topography, drainage, and mode and source of origin.

The Miami silt loam-type of soil, for example, was first mapped in the watershed of the Miami River in Ohio. The soil is gray-brown, with a yellow and gray subsoil. It is neutral to slightly acid in reaction. Its topography is gently rolling, and drainage is fair. The area was invaded by glaciers from the North many thousands of years ago and subsequently covered with forest. The underlying rock is limestone. The "silt loam" signifies that the soil contains a relatively large percentage of particles intermediate in size between the larger sand and the smaller clay sizes.

Other essential land factors besides soil type have to be considered. Thus, at least six classes of slope are now recognized, for slope is often the determining factor in the selection of safe land practices. Almost an equal number of classes of erosion are used, for a severely eroded soil bears little resemblance to one that is well preserved. Soil reaction, salinity, danger of floods, and climatic factors are also considered. The land information thus gathered is placed on a *soil survey map*.

To overcome the complexities of the land pattern and so make the soil map more meaningful to the user, soils are grouped in various ways. The most common and perhaps most useful is the grouping by land capability classes.

In accordance with this concept, all land is made to fall into one of eight classes. These eight classes include two major categories, depending on whether or not they are suitable for controlled cultivation. The division into classes within these two groups is based on the degree to which use is limited by such physical characteristics as slope of the land. Thus land in Classes I, II, III, and IV is normally nearly level, gently sloping, moderately sloping, and strongly sloping, respectively. Class V land is that whose use is limited by such factors as stoniness, dryness, or wetness rather than slope. Classes VI, VII, and VIII contain land that is steep, very steep, and mountainous, respectively.

In addition to slope, excessive wetness, low moisture-holding capacity, and inadequate rainfall may limit land use. Within Class III, for example, is moderately sloping land that needs erosion control, wet land that needs drainage, and sandy land that is limited by low moisture-holding capacity. In some Class III land, the soil is shallow, lying over the tight claypan subsoil. In semiarid regions, much Class III land is of limited value because of lack of rainfall, and constant precaution must be taken against wind erosion.

Once a farm is soil-surveyed and the resulting map is interpreted in accordance with these land-capability classes, the farmer is in position to plan a forward-looking program of land use. The greater the amount of Class I and Class II land, the more intensive the cropping program may be, and the greater the permissible expenditures for machinery and labor. In proportion, as the farm contains more Class III and Class IV land, the farming enterprise would normally be more extensive. In other words, land values and acre yields tend to drop, and larger acreages are necessary for adequate labor incomes in the higher-numbered land classes.

The mere fact that land is placed in one of the higher-numbered classes, however, does not rule it out for profitable farming. In fact, the possibilities may be quite the contrary for men of adaptability. Thus, a well-known Pennsylvania farmer is now operating a highly profitable enterprise of raising heifers for dairy-cow replacement, growing Christmas trees, and producing timber, on 2,500 acres of Class IV, and VI, and VII land, respectively.

Soil survey maps can have great value not only to the farmer and those who advise him but also to many other persons and agencies as well. They are being used in real-estate transactions as a basis for evaluating the land for the purposes that the new owner has in mind. They are also useful in classifying land for taxation, for credit purposes, in condemnation proceedings, and when damages are incurred as a result of highway construction and other public improvements. They are most helpful in connection with sanitary disposal. The New Jersey tax laws require that soil survey maps be considered in the assessment of farm land.

Soil survey maps are also of great value in educating the public to make more profitable use of all the land. There is need not only to conserve the better land for cropping, but also to develop the long-range potentialities of the other land for grazing, forestry, recreational purposes, or wildlife preserves, depending on the use to which it is best adapted. Land-use planners find soil maps an invaluable tool in planning and zoning.

All the People Can Help

Finally, it is now generally recognized that loss of soil is not only bad for the land and bad for the farmer who owns it, but bad for all the people. Loss of productivity is only part of the damage that results. The soil that is carried off the land tends to clog the streams and fill up the storage reservoirs. Every city and most towns have to depend on water that flows by in rivers or is stored in reservoirs behind dams. If the water that is being impounded carries soil in from the surrounding watershed, this soil will soon reduce the storage volume behind the dam. Many such reservoirs are being filled with soil at a rate of 2 or 3 per cent of capacity a year. Thus, in a third to a half of a century, a reservoir may be entirely filled with good topsoil from the surrounding countryside.

A large number of organizations are now devoting a great deal of time and large amounts of money to furthering the cause of conservation. The National Association of Soil Conservation Districts, with offices in League City, Texas, is active in obtaining legislation in support of the better land-use programs sponsored by its members. It is a clearinghouse for information and ideas on district operations. The Soil Conservation Society of America, with offices in Des Moines, Iowa, and over 11,000 members, has state and national meetings to consider conservation problems. It publishes the *Journal of Soil and Water Conservation*. Other national societies are active on behalf of soil, water, forest, and wildlife conservation. All of these, including the Soil Conservation Society of America, are joined in a Natural Resources Council of America, with offices in Washington, D.C.

For the past twelve years the Soil Conservation Society and other land-related organizations have jointly sponsored a watershed congress. Here soil and water leaders gather annually to discuss and promote good watershed treatment and care of the land.

International conservation conferences are not uncommon. The International Soil Science Society meets every four years in a different part of the world. The First Pan American Congress of Soil Conservation was held in São Paulo, Brazil, in April, 1966. The Food and Agriculture Organization of the United Nations is much concerned with care of the soil resources of the world.

Soil conservation is being taught as an undergraduate subject in virtually all of our agricultural colleges. A full conservation curriculum is available at a number of universities. The Universities of Michigan, California, and Minnesota deserve special mention.

Many states and communities have undertaken large- and small-scale conservation programs of various types. Thus, Texas has established the Brazos River Authority, with a six-dam program and the building of a chain of lakes 250 miles long. Ohio has similar authorities for flood control, those operating in the Miami Valley, at Dayton, and in the Muskingum Valley, at Zanesville, having been notably successful. The Stony Brook Watershed Association near Princeton, New Jersey, is an excellent example of what a local community can do to foster soil and water conservation in a rapidly developing area. In addition to working with the Soil Conservation Districts, local municipalities, and the Soil Conservation Service on a nine-dam small watershed project, this organization has spearheaded good land use, community planning, and clean streams in a three-county area.

The aim of all these agencies is not only to stop soil erosion, control floods, protect wildlife, and beautify the country, but also to develop a high sense of appreciation and of responsibility for the soil and our other natural resources. The hope is that when the young people of today have become the leaders of thought and action, they will do a still better job of conserving these resources than their fathers have done.

We have an obligation to make this an ever more beautiful country, where the land is covered with the most useful and luxuriant vegetation to which it is adapted, where gullies are erased, where dust storms are prevented, where flood waters are controlled at their source, and where the streams run clear. Conservation starts around the home, with green grass and attractive flowers and shrubs. It spreads out along the grass-lined highways past vast acreages of carefully cropped fields of corn, wheat, cotton, hay, and pasture land. It extends into the hills and up the mountainsides where luxuriant forests belong. And it permanently preserves large areas of otherwise useless land in all its pristine beauty for our enjoyment.

For Further Reading

BEAR, FIRMAN E. 1962. *Earth, The Stuff of Life.* University of Oklahoma Press, Norman, Oklahoma. 238 pp.

BENNETT, HUGH HAMMOND. 1955. *Elements of Soil Conservation.* McGraw-Hill Book Co., New York. 360 pp.

JOHNSON, V. WEBSTER, and RALEIGH BARLOWE. 1954. *Land Problems and Policies.* McGraw-Hill Book Co., New York. 422 pp.

TREVERT, RICHARD K., *et al.* 1955. *Soil and Water Conservation Engineering.* John Wiley & Sons, Inc., New York. 479 pp.

U.S. Department of Agriculture. *Soil, The 1957 Yearbook of Agriculture.* U.S. Government Printing Office, Washington, D.C. 784 pp.

CHAPTER FOUR

WATER

H. G. Wilm

The Water Resource

A variety of statements can be made to describe water as a natural resource. It is the most universally distributed of resources; it is our most precious and most abundantly available mineral; it is nature's universal solvent for all kinds of material; it has the unusual property of occurring naturally in vapor, liquid, and solid forms; and it is one of mankind's most essential needs.

All of these ideas are true, yet they give hardly a glimpse of the vital importance of water to the people, animals, and plants of the world. From the beginning of time, water has been the key to civilization. Invariably, concentrations of human beings have occurred around the borders of oceans, lakes, and rivers. In short, people need water to live. Without water, they and their communities and their nations cannot survive.

Water is not only our most important servant; it is also one of our greatest enemies. Uncontrolled in the form of floods, water destroys homes, factories, and even whole cities. Water washes away the soil and thus decreases or destroys the fertility of vast areas of land. And when polluted, water brings pestilence to our doorsteps. Thus the relation of people to water is one of constant struggle: to find supplies sufficient to meet human needs, to control floods and erosion, and to minimize the bad effects of pollution.

Complicating the problem is the fact that water supplies are unevenly distributed. In the United States, the average amount of water that falls annually as rain and snow would make a layer about 30 inches deep over the whole country. If this layer were uniform in depth and if the precipitation fell only when it was needed, water problems would be few indeed. But, of course, this happy situation does not occur. Not many places in the United States have more water than they need; and even there the distribution of precipitation is by no means perfect.

Primarily favored with water are two general areas of the United States, the region east of the 95th meridian and the Pacific Northwest. Occupying not much more than one-third of our total land area, these two regions receive fully two-thirds of the total precipitation. In addition, a sizable fraction of the remaining precipitation falls on the great western mountain chains, becoming available only through streamflow to the arid areas below.

Even though total supplies are so unevenly distributed, floods and erosion seem to be almost universal problems. Where precipitation is generally high, large rivers are common, and floods are the product of unusual excesses of water. In more arid regions, rains are likely to occur in the form of high-intensity cloudbursts that cause abrupt floods, of short duration but with great resulting damage. Water pollution occurs practically wherever people live in any important concentrations. Pollution is caused by the dumping of raw or improperly treated sewage into the streams, and by the similar disposal of industrial wastes in excessive quantities. As a result of pollution, the water in many of our rivers is not fit for people or fish to swim in, nor usable for drinking and other domestic purposes until after the water has been thoroughly treated. The people of city after city draw drinking water from the same body of water into which they or other communities have dumped their sewage and their industrial wastes.

Economic and Other Values of Water

For any resource that is so essentially a part of people's lives as is water, it is almost impossible to set an economic value: People pay what they have to for it, and whatever is necessary to keep it under reasonable control and fit for human use. In areas where water is abundant and the demand is low, the selling price of water is correspondingly low. As drawn from streams or ground water it is generally available without charge, and costs the consumer only the expense of development and distribution. In western irrigated areas where the demand is not intense, the cost of water to the consumer is likely to range between $5 and $10 an acre-foot.[1] In other western areas, the cost to agricultural users may be $40 or more; and to large industrial users in similar areas the cost may be $150 to $200 per acre-foot. Even this price is not very great by comparison with that which certain other liquid commodities command.

But still, these figures give only a vague image of the value of water. Perhaps the only true picture of the eco-

---

[1] One acre-foot may be considered as a layer of water one foot deep, spread over one acre of land: 43,560 cubic feet = 326,000 gallons.

nomic value of water can be given by how much people are willing to pay for it as they enter a new area, or just before they have to move out of an established development. *Our Natural Resources and Their Conservation,* by Parkins and Whitaker, contains this interesting statement:

> When gold was discovered in the Australian desert in 1892 and the towns of Kalgoorlie and Collgardie were founded, the district was practically waterless. For a while the railroad transported water to the towns at a cost of about $5000 a day. In 1903 a water line was completed from the Darling range, 350 miles away, and a delivery of 8,000,000 gallons daily resulted. So long are the pipes that they contain a month's supply of water; in other words, the water takes one month in traveling from Mundaring to Kalgoorlie.

Beyond the tangible values of water for direct uses, there are less tangible but fully as important esthetic and recreational values. How much is it worth to preserve or develop a beautiful stream or lake, where people can sail and fish? What is the value of a wilderness tarn, inhabited by beaver and loon, and visited only by an occasional knapsack-laden wanderer? Again, perhaps the only concrete expression is what people are willing to spend or to forego in the way of income to create or preserve such values.

Ecological Relationships

The foregoing suggests the many ways in which water has meaning to people. But up to this point, we have thought of water as an individual resource, separate from its environment. In order to appraise it more fully and to see how water problems may be solved, we have to visualize water as one element in a complex environment involving land, vegetation, animals, and people together.

Let us look briefly at the journey of water from the time it leaves the cloud until it reaches a major river.

What happens to water after it reaches the earth's surface is determined by the character of the watershed land upon which it falls. (The watershed is a land unit bounded by ridges and formed of slopes that direct the flow of water and are drained by a single stream or a single system of streams.) At every step in its passage over or through the watershed to the river, water may be affected in some way by the activities of man. When it first arrives, it may fall on untouched forests, on cut-over woodlots, on pasture or rangeland, or on cultivated fields. If it strikes woodland, a substantial portion of the water is held on the forest canopy and evaporates without reaching the ground. Another portion is absorbed into the soil but returns to the atmosphere by transpiration, through the roots and canopies of the trees. What is left generally goes through the soil in a tranquil manner, appearing later in the form of clear springs and little streams, which join to form clear, healthy rivers.

Water behaves in a similar manner if it falls upon undisturbed grassland, with well-developed root systems and good soil structure, though interception and transpiration may not be as great as in a forest.

When a forest is cut over or burned, however, or grassland is affected by the grazing of animals, these relationships are disturbed. The density and vigor of the vegetation may be substantially reduced. Then the soil structure breaks down until water may run over the surface of the land rather than pass through it to springs and streams. This means accelerated rates of runoff, with more frequent floods and longer periods of low flow during dry weather.

Even more extreme in its effects is the cultivation of land. When forest or grassland is removed and the ground is repeatedly tilled by plow and harrow, inevitably the porous structure of the soil becomes impaired, and water runs increasingly over the surface. After the binding network of plant roots and tops is removed, the soil is exposed to the beating impact of rain and the cutting of rivulets. The result is accelerated runoff, characterized by movement of topsoil, depletion of soil fertility, and the clogging of streams with silt.

When water has reached a stream, whether small or large, it is again affected by man's activities. The character of its movement is affected by the way it came off the land—whether rapidly or slowly, whether through the soil or over the land surface—which in turn depends on whether the land was protected or unprotected by vegetation. Thus, when water reaches a stream, it may flow gently, staying within the stream's banks and carrying little sediment. Or it may come torrentially in abrupt flash floods, often loaded with sediment and debris. Then the streams overtop their channels, destroying fertile bottomlands, tearing out stream banks, and aggravating flood and sediment conditions downstream.

Another factor is pollution. A flowing stream appears to be the simplest way for man to get rid of anything he does not want. Thus the first farmer or miner who builds beside a stream is likely to use it as a dumping-place for trash or offal. Villages do likewise; and the process continues on a larger and larger scale, until great industries and cities virtually destroy rivers and other bodies of water by dumping tremendous volumes of waste material.

But as these bad conditions are created by man's activities, so also can they be remedied by man. On the land, every effort can be made to restore the protective effects of vegetation. Wherever possible, forests can be replanted or restored to good condition. By fertilization, seeding, mowing, and relatively light use, pastures and rangeland can be made to provide watershed protection as well as livestock production. Cultivated lands can be protected by the use of close-growing crops, by contour planting and terracing, by the use of grassed waterways, and by other means of slowing down the movement of water and getting as much as possible into the soil.

A large part of the land area of any watershed is likely to be cultivated. As a consequence, the behavior of streams is likely to be erratic and intermittently destructive. This means that protective work is needed in the streams as well as on the land. Gully checks and small detention dams can be built on the hillsides and in the minor tributaries. In larger streams, storage dams can be used to slow down floods; vegetation, walls, and revetments can be used to protect the banks; and levees can be used to keep the stream within its channel even during floods.

Historical Background

Before we can see how this very general picture of the water resource applies to conditions in the United States, it is essential to look at what conditions were like in colonial days, and how the progressive development of our present civilization has altered and affected the water resource.

When the first colonists reached the east coast of North America, they found an almost untouched wilderness, with hills and valleys clothed in virgin forest. No problems of floods, water supply, or pollution existed at that time. But as the pioneers moved westward into and across the Appalachian Mountains, they cleared great areas of the natural forests, converting them to pasture and cropland. As a result, only half of the original area east of the prairie states is still in forest. The forest and woodlots that are left have been cut over, grazed, and burned, so that a large portion of them are in bad condition. Much of the remaining land in the forest and prairie states has been cleared and cropped, the capacity of the soil to take in water has been reduced, and the result is accelerated runoff and erosion, and flash floods of greater violence in the streams.

Moving westward to escape the increasing pressure of civilization in the East, the first settlers found tremendous areas of plains and mountains. Parts of these western regions are naturally susceptible to high rates of runoff and erosion, and other parts have been overgrazed through the centuries by migrating herds of bison and other game. But most of the mountain lands of the Rockies, Sierra Nevada, and Cascades were in virgin condition, with well-controlled streams and vegetated mountain slopes.

In many western areas these originally good conditions have deteriorated through the cutting of timber, excessive grazing of the rangeland, and poor management of game populations. As a direct consequence, many western mountain stream systems now exhibit the typical characteristics of unhealthy watersheds. And throughout the Great Plains, domestic livestock have perpetuated the conditions created by the original population of game: eroding areas of thin short-grass vegetation, interspersed with cactus and tumbleweed. To top things off, extensive tracts of land in the semiarid Great Plains have been opened to severe wind erosion by the clean cultivation of crops such as wheat.

During this period of land exploitation, the valley areas near the great western rivers have been continuously developed into productive irrigated cropland. Also, these streams have made possible the growth of wealthy cities and industries. All this agricultural and urban development has brought about a progressively intensifying demand for water, until now the needs exceed available supplies in many western areas.

The obvious deterioration of land and water under man's use has long compelled far-seeing men to raise voices of warning. Even in colonial times, men like Washington and Jefferson commented on the erosion problems associated with cultivation. Later the voices of other men such as George P. Marsh, R. B. Hough, Gifford Pinchot, and Hugh H. Bennett were raised in increasing numbers, until finally the growth of public consciousness led to a nationwide movement for soil and water conservation.

With this movement came federal laws intended to help protect and develop land and water resources. The Acts of 1891 and 1897 authorized the reservation of public lands as forest reserves, and provided that "no public reservation shall be established except to improve and protect the forest within the reservation or for the purpose of securing favorable conditions of water flows and to furnish a continuous supply of timber." These laws were followed in 1905 by the establishment of the Forest Service in the U.S. Department of Agriculture, and in 1911 by the Weeks Law, which provided for the protection of the watersheds of navigable streams.

In the arid West, the use of water for irrigation was advanced by the Reclamation Act of 1902, which provided specifically for the development of lands for irrigated agriculture. Under the provisions of this act with later amendments, and through widespread private initiative, many millions of acres of otherwise arid and unproductive land have been transformed to a high degree of value and productivity throughout the West; and even greater developments are envisioned for the future.

These activities and laws provided especially for the development and protection of forested watersheds and of western irrigated land. In the meantime, there also arose a demand for the conservation of land and water in the more settled areas of the United States, where cultivation exerts a dominant influence. An important goal was reached with the establishment of the Soil Erosion Service, later renamed the Soil Conservation Service, in 1933, and passage of the Soil Conservation Act of 1935. This act was designed to provide for "the control and prevention of soil erosion and thereby to preserve natural resources, control floods, prevent impairment of reservoirs, maintain the navigability of rivers and harbors, protect public health and public lands, and relieve unemployment."

Soon after that time the Omnibus Flood Control Act of 1936 (with subsequent amendments) established the nationwide interest of the federal government in flood control. This act authorized the Secretary of the Army (through the Corps of Engineers) to make investigations and surveys of flood problems in the rivers of the United States. It also provided that the Secretary of Agriculture should make investigations and institute programs on watersheds for the purpose of runoff and waterflow retardation and soil-erosion prevention.

Aside from several years' break during World War II, the Forest Service and Soil Conservation Service conducted surveys and administered remedial programs on watersheds under this Act until 1954. The action programs are continuing; but at that time other work by the Department of Agriculture under the Flood Control Act was superseded by activities under the Small Watershed Act, Public Law 566, enacted in 1954 and subsequently amended many times. This act provides, among other things:

> . . . that the Federal Government should cooperate with States and their political subdivisions, soil or water conservation districts, flood prevention or control districts, and other local public agencies for the purpose of preventing such damages (that is, from erosion, flood water, and sediment in the watersheds of the rivers and streams of the United States) and of furthering the conservation, development, utilization, and disposal of water and thereby of preserving and protecting the nation's land and water resources.

Specifically the Secretary of Agriculture is authorized, upon application from local organizations:

1. to conduct such investigations and surveys as may be necessary to prepare plans for works of improvement;
2. to make such studies as may be necessary for determining the physical and economic soundness of plans for works of improvement, including a determination as to whether benefits exceed costs;
3. to cooperate and enter into agreements with and to furnish financial and other assistance to local organizations. . . .
4. to obtain the cooperation and assistance of other federal agencies in carrying out the purposes of this section.

One feature of this act deserves special emphasis: It is pointed at local problems on small watersheds, and at their solution by local organizations assisted by the states and federal government. This means a real step forward in the improvement of watershed conditions, because it supports the spontaneous work of local people on their own personal problems, with any guidance that they may need.

Other laws of importance to the water user have to do

with water pollution problems. In 1948 was passed the first Federal Water Pollution Act, which recognized the rights of the states in controlling water pollution. This Act also provided for financial assistance by the federal government and a certain degree of legal pressure. Since 1948, much constructive progress has been made by a number of states in the abatement of serious pollution problems. This progress has been greatly accelerated by the passage of several amendments, including the Water Pollution Act of 1965 and 1966, that have provided progressively stronger mechanisms for achieving interstate pollution control. Even now, however, a tremendous task lies ahead. In New York State alone, it is estimated that adequate control of water pollution will require expenditure of at least $1.7 billion by municipalities, the State of New York, and the federal government. In addition, it is estimated that the adequate regulation of industrial pollution will require the private investment of another $100 million.

Current Watershed Program

During the past three centuries our country has grown from a restricted group of settlements on the eastern seaboard, with primitive pioneer conditions, to a continent-wide civilization of tremendous wealth and resources. As we have seen, this development has taken a severe toll in resource depletion. But the situation has its bright side too. Perhaps because of the very severity of this depletion, it has developed a strong counteracting movement on a number of fronts.

One of the first of these was the establishment of the national forests under the Forest Service of the U.S. Department of Agriculture. Elsewhere in the federal government, the U.S. Army's Corps of Engineers is engaged in large-scale flood control activities on the major rivers of the country. In the West, the Department of the Interior's Bureau of Reclamation is developing and planning major projects for irrigation and power that will greatly increase the productivity of arid lands. And the Soil Conservation Service of the Department of Agriculture sponsors a program of soil and water conservation that goes a long way toward stabilizing the productivity of croplands.

Several other agencies and kinds of work deserve special mention, as they play an essential role in watershed improvement. First are the extension services of the various states, together with the Extension Service of the U.S. Department of Agriculture. These have traditionally rendered valuable services through the teaching of better methods of land management and conservation. Other services to watershed people are direct financial aids supplied through the Agricultural Stabilization and Conservation Service and financial credit supplied through the Farmers' Home Administration.

Aside from the widespread federal activities, many states are active in soil and water conservation through water conservation boards, resource conservation divisions, state foresters, and similar agencies. These cooperate with both the federal government and private organizations and individuals.

In a kind of work that will be of special significance to many readers of this book, individuals interested in conservation are increasingly banding themselves together into more or less formal organizations for the promotion of soil and water conservation. Those of national scope include associations dedicated particularly to the protection and improvement of forest land; to soil and water conservation in general, but especially on agricultural land; to the preservation and management of wildlife; to the reclamation and development of arid western lands; to the establishment and preservation of wilderness areas; and to other important purposes.

Of the many kinds of more local organizations, those worth special mention are watershed associations and similar organizations designed to protect, rehabilitate, and develop the land and water resources of relatively local areas. Among the older and better known of these are the Brandywine Valley Association in Delaware, and the Miami and Muskingum Conservancy Districts in Ohio. Another is the Connecticut River Watershed Council, which ties together watershed activities in that whole river system and contains several active watershed associations on tributaries to the Connecticut River. All these and similar organizations and areas are worth the study of anyone who is interested in watershed improvement. They are doing good work, which is greatly facilitated by the guidance and assistance provided under the Watershed Protection and Flood Prevention Act.

A watershed association is simply an organization of people resident in a watershed who desire to make the area a better place to live and work. Watershed associations have brought about improvements in the social and economic conditions of the people through the restoration and conservation of the natural resources. In short, a watershed association provides a meeting ground where people can plan and unite for community improvement of soil, water, and related resources.

Where watershed problems and damages are intimately related to each other in a small area, a local or "community-size" watershed may be quite limited in extent—occasionally as small as ten square miles or so. In other localities, especially in the West, such watersheds are necessarily much larger. Because both the damaging flood waters and the essential water supplies come from mountain lands, remote from the valley cities and farms, a single watershed unit may need to include a thousand or more square miles. And even then it may be necessary to provide some mechanism for coordinating work in a series of watersheds whose problems are related to each other. In the Colorado River Drainage Basin, for example, water produced in the Wyoming Rockies is used as far away as California and Mexico. Therefore, water development for irrigation or other purposes anywhere in the Basin has a direct or indirect effect upon people somewhere else in the Basin.

These facts indicate the need for plans and action programs prepared for whole drainage basins as well as for smaller areas. The federal government has set the stage for such work through the preparation of plans for several major basins of the United States: the New England–New York area, the Arkansas–Red–White River Basins in the central and southern states, and the Missouri River and Columbia River Basins. Plans for these areas have been prepared under the leadership of the federal agencies interested in water resource development, with participation of representatives of the several states involved in each basin. These efforts have been only partially successful, because of the great complexity of the problems in any major basin and the interlocking and often conflicting interests of the various people and agencies involved. But while the planning cannot be considered perfect in itself, it has provided a valuable meeting ground for the development of interagency cooperation. And it points up the basic fact that basin-wide integration of water resource development is essential. If it cannot be achieved by cooperative endeavors such as these basin plans, more powerful administrative tools are required. Such a tool has now been provided by the adoption of the Delaware River Basin Compact of 1961, through which the states of New York, New Jersey, Pennsylvania, and Delaware have banded together in partnership with the federal government for the planning and administration of water resources. The commission established under this compact has almost unique powers, and is further unusual in that the federal government is represented by a single member appointed by the President; the other members are the governors of the four states. The wisdom and strength of this compact were amply demonstrated during the dry season of 1965, following three earlier seasons of severe drought in the Northeast.

Direct education and research supply two effective weapons for water resource conservation and management. In education, elementary and high schools are increasingly including conservation as a part of their programs. The technical subjects of hydraulics and water engineering, hydrology, and watershed management are taught at a number of colleges and universities; and most of the accredited schools of forestry in the United States offer instruction in forest influences and watershed management.

A substantial body of new knowledge is being obtained from research, principally by federal and state agencies. The U.S. Forest Service has a well-organized group of watershed studies. Although the Soil Conservation Service is primarily an "action" agency, much valuable knowledge of watershed hydrology has been obtained from its soil and water research, which was transferred in 1954 to the Agricultural Research Service of the Department of Agriculture. Smaller programs of research have been or are being carried on by the Geological Survey, Department of the Interior, by the U.S. Weather Bureau, and by universities and state experiment stations. These comments apply particularly to research on watershed rehabilitation, management, and improvement. In addition, much useful research has been conducted by federal agencies, universities, and other organizations on the direct control of water and on water pollution.

An outstanding example is the Waterways Experiment Station of the U.S. Corps of Engineers at Vicksburg, Mississippi, where skillfully controlled experiments are conducted on the design of dams and other channel structures and on the hydrology of major rivers such as the Mississippi. This world-famous station conducts experiments on stream flow. Exact-scale working models of various river and harbor systems, including the entire Mississippi basin, have been installed. Research on the design of dams and other channel structures is carried on. Through such experiments the destructive effects of floods may be lessened, the quantity of silt in water may be reduced, and the volume of water flow may be regulated.

All these activities aim at improving watersheds and existing water supplies. A different kind of work is intended to increase water supplies by attacking the clouds themselves. "Cloud-seeding" has been greatly advertised and hardly needs description. It involves adding to masses of moist air particles of some finely divided material such as silver iodide that "coagulates" the vapor into precipitable droplets. Such a process is theoretically possible and has been demonstrated under controlled conditions. On a large, practical scale many millions of dollars have been and are being spent by farmers, industries, and others on commercial cloud-seeding contracts and experiments. As yet, however, unbiased and controlled tests have failed to demonstrate any real effect of cloud-seeding on aerial precipitation.

The Tasks That Lie Ahead

In spite of all the current programs, the nation is obviously still plagued by water shortages, floods, sediment, and pollution. Current work by individuals, local organizations, universities, and state and federal agencies needs to be continued and expanded. Because our knowledge of sound management practices is still sketchy, emphasis needs to be placed especially on research in watershed management, hydrology, and meteorology, including cloud-seeding.

It is hard to suggest what any individual can contribute. The least he can do, of course, is to become informed on these problems and to let his public servants know what he wants. More concretely, he can help organize and become an active member of a local or regional organization such as a watershed association, assuming whatever role is appropriate to his background of training and experience. If he is a landowner he can work continuously toward the improvement of his holdings, for the benefit of his own family as well as that of his neighbors downstream, and with any necessary guidance and assistance from a watershed association or other agency.

Whatever he does, one thing is certain: There is a constructive job for everyone in the very great task of water management, watershed improvement, flood control, and pollution abatement that still lies ahead. This is no light or casual duty. The history of dead civilizations tells only too tragically what our future may be if we neglect this task.

For Further Reading

COLMAN, E. A. 1953. *Vegetation and Watershed Management.* The Ronald Press Co., New York. 412 pp.

FRANK, BERNARD, and ANTHONY NETBOY. 1950. *Water, Land, and People.* Alfred A. Knopf, Inc., New York. 331 pp.

HOYT, WILLIAM G., and WALTER B. LANGBEIN. 1955. *Floods.* Princeton University Press, Princeton, N.J. 469 pp.

HUFFMAN, ROY E. 1953. *Irrigation Development and Public Water Policy.* The Ronald Press Co., New York. 336 pp.

LEOPOLD, LUNA, and THOMAS MADDOCK, JR. 1954. *The Flood Control Controversy.* The Ronald Press Co., New York. 278 pp.

MARSH, GEORGE P. 1874. *The Earth as Modified by Human Action.* Scribner, Armstrong & Co., New York.

PARKINS, A. E., and J. R. WHITAKER (eds.). 1936. *Our Natural Resources and Their Conservation.* John Wiley & Sons, Inc., New York. 650 pp.

President's Water Resources Policy Commission. 1950. *A Water Policy for the American People.* U.S. Government Printing Office, Washington, D.C. 445 pp.

THOMAS, HAROLD E. 1951. *The Conservation of Ground Water.* McGraw-Hill Book Co., New York. 327 pp.

WILM, H. G. 1953. Foresters in the Watershed Movement. *American Forests* 61:28 ff.

CHAPTER FIVE

GRASSLANDS

David F. Costello

From primitive times to the present, man's history has been largely influenced by grasslands. Civilization began on the grasslands. Civilizations have vanished through destructions of grasslands. One-third of the land area of the world is still classified as range, or natural grassland of relatively large extent, where livestock are grazed.

The Original Grasslands

Of the 1.904 billion acres that comprise the total area of the United States, about one-third originally was grassland, while the remainder consisted of forests, deserts, barren rock, rivers, lakes, and tundra. Even in the open forests and on the more productive desert lands, additional millions of acres supported grass as an understory to the trees or shrubs, and this grass was valuable forage for game animals or livestock.

The original grasslands of the United States were characterized by grasses and herbs primarily useful as forage and soil-holding cover. The breadstuffs of the world—barley, wheat, rye, corn, millet, and rice—became important as cultivation prepared the soil for their growth. Likewise, the pasture and lawn grasses, such as redtop, orchard grass, Kentucky bluegrass, creeping bent, and red fescue came into wide use as farms and cities spread across the continent.

The different plants, of which there were thousands in the original grasslands, thrived under varied conditions of soil and climate. Some were restricted to certain localities such as salt marshes or alpine summits. Others, such as the sod-forming buffalograss, occurred throughout the Great Plains over areas of thousands of square miles. Some were annuals, which grew for a single season and reproduced only by seed. Most were perennials that persisted for many seasons.

Soil-holding grasses such as quackgrass and beach grass grew from rhizomes or underground stems. Sod-formers, such as blue grama and buffalograss, were low-growing plants that resisted trampling by grazing animals. Bunchgrasses, such as the fescues and three-awns, grew in scattered tufts that enabled them to take advantage of limited soil moisture during the summer growing season. Each species had its own characteristic reproductive rate and its own endurance to grazing.

Forage value of grasses, herbs, and shrubs varied. Some were sought eagerly, others were grazed indifferently, and many were avoided by game animals and livestock. The short grasses of the Great Plains were palatable the year around. Many annual grasses were palatable only for a few weeks in spring. A few kinds of grasses were avoided because of their lack of taste or their spiny seed heads. Likewise, wide differences in the nutritive value of forage plants—variations in protein content and mineral level from season to season and from species to species—contributed to the variations in the original grasslands of America.

In the East, the major grasslands were the prairies of the Central and Lake States, and scattered savannahs in the breaks of the primeval hardwood forests. The native upland species at the time of settlement included big bluestem, little bluestem, Indiangrass, porcupine grass, prairie sandgrass, and sand dropseed. These were palatable to grazing animals in summer but did not cure well for winter forage. Important in the lowlands were American sloughgrass, the mannagrasses, common reedgrass, and prairie cordgrass. These furnished much of the native hay during the early years of settlement, while the uplands were being plowed and seeded to grain crops and to introduced clovers, timothy, redtop, and bluegrasses.

In the South, grasslands of relatively limited extent occurred on the Gulf Coast, on the black lands of Mississippi and Alabama, and in the marshes and Everglades of Florida. The coastal prairies were characterized by tall, coarse grasses, sedges, and rushes. In the fresh-water marshes of Florida, salt grass was the dominant species. Marshgrass occupied areas inundated by salt water at high tide. These rank grasses, taller than a man's head, provided nutritious forage during the growing season.

In the rest of the nation, the principal grassland types were the tall-grass prairies of the Midwest; the mixed prairie or short-grass plains east of the Rockies; the semi-desert grasslands of the Southwest, and the Pacific bunchgrass lands, which occurred in the Northwest and in the Central Valley of California. Where these types occurred west of the 100th meridian, they were a part of the western range, which still constitutes three-fourths of the range area of the United States.

The tall-grass prairies were dominated by the highly prized bluestems, which grew in mixture with goldenrods, wild daisies, the wreath aster, and other showy herbs. On sandy uplands the lead plant or "prairie shoestring" was conspicuous. Abundant grasses of lesser importance were the needlegrasses, sideoats grama, switchgrass, and the bunch-forming sand dropseed.

The prairie was the most productive of all the grassland types and had high recuperative power under a rainfall that varied from 20 inches in the Dakotas to more than 40 inches in the lush bluestem prairies of the Flint Hills and Osage areas of Kansas and Oklahoma. The prairie grasses were most valuable for summer grazing, since they did not cure well for fall and winter use.

The short-grass range, largest of the grassland types, extended from the Texas Panhandle northward into Canada and eastward from the Rocky Mountains into the Dakotas, Nebraska, and Kansas. Grasses of low stature, the gramas, buffalograss, western wheatgrass, and needle-and-thread produced nutritious forage in spring and early summer. When cured on the stalk, they furnished valuable winter grazing.

Pacific bunchgrass prairie in Montana, Washington, Idaho, Oregon, and central California resembled the prairies of the Midwest, but the plant species were different. The characteristic bluebunch wheatgrass, Idaho fescue, and California needlegrass were well adapted to the long dry summers and wet winters. Abundant forage was palatable when green, but it was relatively low in value during the winter season.

Semidesert grasslands of the Southwest contained a mixture of highly nutritious grasses, broadleaved herbs, and scattered shrubs and trees that provided forage the year around. Under near-desert conditions, black grama, dropseeds, tobosa grass, alkali sacaton, and three-awns predominated. At higher elevations where scattered trees and numerous varieties of shrubs bordered the desert, grama grasses, curly mesquite, and dropseeds were abundant. Grazing capacity was moderate, and heavy grazing easily reduced the range to barrenness in this vast area of low rainfall.

The sagebrush-grass type of vegetation, which occurred on 90 million acres in the West, provided forage in spring, fall, and winter for animals that migrated from the high-mountain summer ranges. Originally the sagebush-grass types was rich in associated species, particularly the wheatgrasses, fescues, needlegrasses, Indian ricegrass, wild geranium, balsamroot, phlox, and bitterbrush. It was susceptible to misuse by livestock because of its accessibility and the semiarid country in which it grew.

Many other areas in the West produced abundant grass in their primitive conditions. At moderate elevations, above the sagebrush and desert zones, woodland types prevailed. Here, wheatgrasses, bromes, and palatable shrubs such as mountain mahogany formed understories beneath pinyons, junipers, or oaks. At still higher elevations, open forests of pine, Douglas-fir, aspen, and spruce were intermingled with meadows and grassy areas highly desirable for summer grazing by big-game animals and livestock.

In all this vast range area of the nation, a magnificent and renewable vegetation resource awaited the coming of white man. When he began his conquest, he little realized the value of grasslands as producers of forage, wildlife, timber, water, and recreation for man's physical and spiritual welfare.

Grasslands of Today

The freedom and vastness of the American frontier have vanished under the pressure of modern agricultural methods, swift transportation, and the growth of cities, villages, and rural homes. Now the original tall-grass prairies are farmlands. The better sodlands of the South and of the Pacific Northwest have been plowed. Millions of acres in the arid West and Southwest are used for irrigated crops. The western range is the single remaining large area of natural grazing land. It remains as a residue of the original grasslands because of its physical or economic unsuitability for other agricultural uses.

Since 1880, acreage of grazing lands in the United States has declined more than 300 million acres, mostly at the expense of the open range. This decline does not represent the entire shift from native range to cropland, since plowed land is constantly being shifted to permanent planted pastures. In general, however, the better lands have remained in cultivation, and the poorer lands have been left in range.

In the country as a whole more than a billion acres are still being grazed. Of this acreage, about 633 million acres are permanent grasslands; 320 million acres are woodlands and forest, grazed at least part of the year; and the remainder includes croplands and planted fields that are pastured by livestock. More than one-third of the livestock feed in the nation is produced on pastures and grazing lands.

Man's Use of the Grasslands

Although the nation's grasslands support a large and important livestock industry, they also afford protection to watersheds, produce countless game animals, and provide space for millions of recreationists. Their vegetation cover is essential in the reduction of siltation in reservoirs, lowering of flood hazards, and preservation of habitat for fish and waterfowl. Through multiple use, grasslands are basic to individual, community, and public welfare.

It is almost impossible to place an average value on the products of grasslands. An acre of range in the West may produce only 10 pounds of beef per year, as contrasted with 2,000 pounds per acre produced by improved pastures in Florida. But a population of 90 million cattle and an annual value that recently has approached $15 billion for beef and animal products indicate the economic importance of grasslands in the United States. Even in the 17 western states, where land values are relatively low, if we assume a valuation of $10 per acre, the grazing lands would be worth nearly $8 billion. Reliable estimates are not available for the value of wildlife produced, or for the water that flows from the land and is used for power, irrigation, manufacturing, and urban consumption.

RECREATIONAL AND ESTHETIC BENEFITS. Man has never completely divested himself of his primitive urge to associate with natural surroundings. That urge can be satisfied in part by outdoor recreation, which not only gives physiological benefit but meets his psychological needs and changes his spiritual outlook.

The search for recreational release has been intensified by population pressure, more leisure hours per year, improved transportation, income above subsistence needs, acceptance of the vacation idea, and the development of recreation as a major industry. The value of recreation and the outdoor life can be judged by the intensity with which men pursue it. More than 14 million people annually buy hunting licenses, and approximately 20 million buy fishing licenses; more than 250 million visits are annually recorded for the national forests, parks, and monuments; uncounted numbers go on local picnics, swim in not-too-clean water, enjoy bird watching, take nature hikes, or simply view the natural world for its inspirational beauty.

Herein lies part of the importance of the grasslands in general and the western range in particular. Millions are beginning to weigh the proportionate benefits of beefsteaks and spiritual stimulation, of "No Trespassing" signs and release from nervous tension, of smog and tonic climate, and of misuse of the land and planned ecological management. The tragedy of the past is that the recreational areas of the East are inadequate or have been diverted to other uses by the encroachment of agriculture, industry, and urban development. The hope of the future is that the importance of western public land will be recognized in time to preserve and restore the recreational resources of grasslands and forests that the automobile, streamlined train, and airplane now place within reach of a large segment of the nation's people.

ECOLOGICAL RELATIONSHIPS. Much of grassland and range management is merely applied plant ecology, which deals with the response of soil and vegetation to the grazing of animals and other influences. From the fund of ecological knowledge, we are able to reconstruct what grasslands have been in the past and to predict what they may be in the future.

Ecology deals both with single species and with communities of species. Both are important on the range.

The continued existence of vegetation depends upon completion of the life cycles of individual plants. Disturbances in the life cycles of plants are the ultimate causes of change in range condition and productivity, and therefore the source of most problems in range management.

By growing in groups, plants produce vegetation. Owing to diversities in environment, plant groups develop into associations having overall characteristics that make them recognizable as distinct communities or range types. Communities replace or succeed one another in progressive or retrogressive series leading either to optimum vegetation cover or to depleted and unproductive range. Herein lies the application of ecology to range management. Through knowledge of vegetation dynamics, the range manager can control the growth of individual plants and thereby manipulate plant succession to provide optimum forage production and provide for related and other uses of the land.

Let us consider a plant community that has been destroyed and that can be restored through proper application of ecological knowledge. In recent years, more than 20 million acres of short-grass range have been plowed in the Great Plains. The original blue grama and buffalograss sod and its multitude of associated plants —wheatgrasses, dropseeds, asters, cactus, and various low-growing shrubs—have been wholly or partly eliminated by continuous crop-growing on thousands of farms.

Many of these areas never should have been plowed. Cultivation has been abandoned on thousands of acres, with the result that all stages of recovery now are present, from nearly bare fields to remnants of original grassland. Under good management, this conversion from bare ground and weedy fields to short-grass range can be made

to proceed satisfactorily while the lands are being grazed.
Several well-defined stages in vegetation development
occur in the process of conversion to range land. In the
first years after cultivation has ceased, nearly pure stands
of annual weeds appear. This stage, consisting of Russian
thistles, sunflowers, lambsquarters, and pigweeds, is inevitable, since the site is unprepared for growth of more
desirable plants. Use of the land should be deferred for
three or four years until this stage of development has
passed; livestock grazing may simply prolong the stage
for 20 years or more.

A perennial weed stand normally replaces the annual
weeds. Species of low palatability, such as scarlet globe-
mallow, tansyleaf aster, curlycup gumweed, silky sophora,
and horseweed fleabane, normally occupy the area for
three to six years. When grazed lightly, in combination
with adjoining native grasslands, these weedy areas furnish nutritive forage that balances the grass herbage in the
livestock diet. But grazing of weed stages should be deferred until late summer to avoid destructive grazing of
invading grasses in their seedling and early growth stages.

Various low- or moderate-value grasses normally make
their appearance in the perennial weed stand within 5 to
10 years after abandonment of cultivation. Such grasses
as sand dropseed, western wheatgrass, and Indian ricegrass are the principal grasses in this stage and are a part
of the transition to a more permanent grass cover.

A grass stage more or less dominated by the tuft-form-
ing grass, red three-awn, usually develops within 15 to 20
years following the last cultivation. Short grasses then
slowly invade over the next 20 to 30 years. The final vegetation stage is characterized by development of blue
grama and buffalograss sod. Various taller grasses and a

variety of perennial weeds and shrubs also become established in the short-grass community. Once it is restored, conservative grazing thereafter is essential to its perpetuation.

The ecological approach is also basic to rational classification of range condition. When range condition classes are described in terms of successional stages of plant communities, we have a basis for describing the range, for measuring its trend of deterioration or improvement, and for estimating its yield in terms of animal production and economic return.

Here is one example of the relationship between range condition and cattle weight gains on ponderosa pine–bunchgrass range, based on experiments at the Manitou Experimental Forest near Woodland Park, Colorado. It was estimated that one square mile of range in excellent range condition could produce more than 11,000 pounds of beef gain per year. Good-condition ranges could produce 7,300 pounds, fair ranges 4,600 pounds, and poor ranges only 2,500 pounds. The question immediately arises, "How can a poor range be made into a fair range, a fair one into a good one, or a good one into an excellent one?" The answer lies in ecological principles that can be applied in terms of proper seasons of grazing, proper distribution of grazing, proper kind and class of livestock, and proper numbers of animals. The need for application of these principles becomes apparent when we consider that more than half of the rangelands of the nation are in little better than fair condition.

History

EARLY EXPLORATION AND ABUSES. The story of expansion of the livestock industry and abuse of the nation's grasslands can be told briefly. Columbus, on his second voyage, landed the first livestock on the continent in 1493. Coronado and his conquistadors brought the first horses, mules, cattle, sheep, and hogs into the Southwest in 1540. Other expeditions from Mexico soon followed, and with the establishment of the Franciscan missions in northern Mexico and California and the introduction of livestock at St. Augustine, Florida, in 1565, and later at Jamestown colony and along the Delaware River in the East, the movement of domestic grazing animals into the interior of an unexplored continent began in earnest.

Western livestock production swiftly expanded after 1830 when eastern producers met the Texas trail herds moving northward. Diminishing opposition from the Indians, extension of railroad systems, and stimulation of marketing by the California gold rush and the Civil War set the stage for the greatest livestock boom in history. By 1890, there were 26 million cattle and 20 million sheep in the 17 western states, and the once "inexhaustible" range was fully stocked.

The conquest of the grasslands continued. Fierce competition for forage by cattlemen and sheepmen led to open war on the range. Conservation of the resource was completely disregarded. Grass was free, and belonged to the man who got there first with the most livestock and grazed the closest. Overexpansion, lack of management, ignorance, greed, and absence of supervision and control led inevitably to prodigal exploitation and depletion.

Bitter experience slowly indicated the need for management and regulation of use on the range. The terrible winter of 1886 killed animals by the million. Prolonged drought followed, and again blizzards almost eliminated the herds. Then came the settlers with their plows and their barbed wire fences. Farms and cities grew westward, millions of citizens settled on the land, and grassland use in America, early in the twentieth century, finally entered an era in which planning and improved management became imperative.

CAUSES OF DEPLETION. The world history of grazing has been one of declining productivity of natural grasslands. But nowhere has the decline occurred so swiftly as in the United States. Within half a century, the grazing capacity of the original range decreased by more than 50 per cent. The cause was simple—too many cows and too many sheep. But the earmarks of depletion, although apparent, were not understood, or were ignored.

Palatable perennial grasses of desert, plain, and mountain were grazed beyond their ability to recuperate. Their vigor decreased, they failed to produce seed, and the resulting thinned plant cover permitted wind and water erosion, loss of topsoil, gully formation, lowering of water tables, drying up of streams, flash floods, and siltation of lakes and rivers. Palatable shrubs suffered in the same respects. Low-value annual grasses, worthless shrubs, and noxious weeds increased alarmingly where productive grassland had once flourished. Depletion occurred under all conditions of climate, topography, and land ownership. Local overstocking resulted in a lack of balance in the supply of year-round forage. Shortages of winter feed on the deserts created demands for greater and earlier use of spring range in the foothills and, later, for use of summer range in the high mountains. Thus overuse was pushed to the last frontiers of the range.

Improper grazing also resulted from lack of knowledge on the part of old-world farmer immigrants unaccustomed to the management of arid and semiarid lands. At the same time, the homestead laws limited available acreages to less than a tenth of the area necessary for sustained economic livestock production. Then federal reservations of the public domain brought increasing restrictions. The end of free range and a nationwide scarcity of grass were in sight.

Rise of the Conservation Movement

Recognition of the need for conservation of resources has always followed the pinch of scarcity. It is the old story of not missing the water until the well goes dry. In the history of our country, eastern forest resources became limited long before the grasslands of the West were exploited. Consequently, the importance of preservation of trees led to the earliest movements for sustained production of natural products of the land.

EARLIEST LAWS AND PROGRAMS. William Penn, recognizing a scarcity of building timber, signed an ordinance in 1681 providing that every fifth acre should be left uncut when the forest was cleared. President John Quincy Adams established a naval station near Pensacola, Florida, in 1828, to preserve a supply of live oak for the construction of battleships. With advance of the nineteenth century, the nature of resource values and depletion were more generally recognized. Yellowstone National Park was created by Congress in 1872. The American Association for the Advancement of Science memorialized Congress in 1873 to pass laws leading to conservation. The American Forestry Association, in recognition of the need for better management of timber lands, was formed in 1875.

These philosophies and actions were superimposed on a changing national land policy. Beginning in colonial days, through cessions of state claims, treaties with England, the Louisiana Purchase, and other transactions, the United States acquired title to its vast holdings of public land. Following acquisition, lands were sold to obtain revenue, to encourage settlement, and to further internal improvements through grants to the states for educational purposes, and to the railroads for westward expansion. Many of these state and railroad lands eventually passed into private ownership.

Depletion of timber and grazing resources awakened progressive individuals and agencies to the need for conservation through retention of the remaining public lands and by federal administration. In 1891, the first forest reserve was established in President Harrison's administration. This was the turning point in the conservation of public lands. By 1909, Presidents Harrison, Cleveland, and Theodore Roosevelt had set aside additional reserves totaling 148 million acres. In 1954, there were 179 million acres of national forest land in the continental United States. It was not until 1934, however, that the unregulated lands of the remaining public domain were placed under management by passage of the Taylor Grazing Act. These lands, now under jurisdiction of the Bureau of Land Management, total 180 million acres. Establishment of national forests and of federal grazing districts finally terminated free use of the range and brought controlled use involving payment for the privilege of grazing on public property.

RANGE MANAGEMENT BECOMES A SCIENCE. Organization of the national forests in 1905 crystallized the need for quantitative methods in the regulation of grazing for maintenance and improvement of the range. Prior to 1900 the demands for research were few and studies were merely exploratory, involving the discovering and description of native plants. Limited intensive studies were made from 1905 to 1909, principally by A. W. Sampson and James T. Jardine, with emphasis on habits of sheep and growth requirements of vegetation. Their studies led to better methods of sheep-herding, stock water development, deferred and rotation grazing, and other improvements, including range surveys.

Organized grazing experiments were started throughout the mountainous West and the Great Plains from 1910 to 1926. These experiments included studies of grazing in relation to erosion and floods, eradication of poisonous plants, tests of natural revegetation, and range reseeding trials.

The great impetus to range research came with the establishment of a research branch in the Forest Service in 1926 and with the passage of the McSweeney-McNary Forest Research Act in 1928, which provided for studies by forest and range experiment stations. Under these stations, important field branches were organized, including the Desert Experimental Range in western Utah, the San Joaquin Experimental Range in central California, the Central Plains Experimental Range in northern Colorado, and the Starkey Experimental Forest and Range in eastern Oregon. At present, research also is being done in range management, range reseeding, range livestock production, and related fields by the Agricultural Research Service, the Bureau of Plant Industry, Soils, and Agricultural Engineering, Soil Conservation Service nurseries, the Bureau of Animal Industry, the Fish and Wildlife

Service, and all of the western state agricultural experiment stations. Additional interest in the science of grazing land management has been created by the formation of the American Society of Range Management, in 1947.

Range research in the past 50 years has built up a large body of scientific knowledge applicable to the restoration of depleted forage, the maintenance of ranges in good condition, handling of livestock for optimum production of animal products, protection of watersheds, and integration with other land usage, including forestry, big-game production, and recreation. Experiments with 2,4-D and other herbicides now enable the range manager to control many poisonous and noxious plants on the range. Methods of artificial seeding have been developed for range types through tests of adaptability of hundreds of native and introduced plants. The researcher can now tell the range operator not only what grass seeds to plant, but where to plant, when to plant, how much to plant, how deep to plant, what machinery to use, and finally, how to graze the artificially produced grassland.

Research on food reserves in forage plants has provided a scientific basis for restoring depleted ranges through systems of management such as short-season grazing, deferred grazing, and rotation grazing. It is now known, for example, that spring growth of grass is related to the amount of carbohydrates stored in the roots. Likewise, food reserves fluctuate with the rate of plant growth, with flower and seed production, and with the amount of herbage removed by grazing animals. Thus, better understanding of the physiological requirements of plants has resulted in more specific recommendations for proper seasons of use, proper numbers and kinds of animals, and proper distribution of animals on the range.

The need for research is still increasing. Changing biological conditions, such as the recent upsurge of big-game animals on the range, present new problems. Are deer and elk, for example, competitive or compatible with livestock? Changing economics and social conditions are also presenting range production problems of increasing complexity. The changing pattern of land use and the increasing demand for multiple products from the same areas are producing additional problems for modern land managers. We will obtain the answers only if we intensify and expand our programs of research.

It is important that we look at how we are expanding and contracting our programs of research. Nationally, we are preoccupied with outer-space and atomic investigations to the neglect of research on the land. In natural resource research, disproportionate amounts of money, in relation to product values, are being spent, for example, on forestry and agricultural chemical studies. Government agencies are concentrating grassland research at fewer locations and are de-emphasizing field study in the natural environment. The relatively few competent scientists are being made into executives, and technicians are being designated as "scientists." In the universities, teachers are devoting more time to teaching and less to research training and supervision because of increasing student enrollment.

On the plus side, multipurpose research is increasing. The more imaginative researchers are combining their efforts with those of workers from other disciplines so that recreation, wildlife production, watershed protection, and livestock grazing are receiving occasional integrated study. A few scientists hope that this interdisciplinary research will result in improved knowledge of our complex and dynamic grassland ecosystems.

Modern Practices and Concepts

Livestock operations throughout the vast range and pasture area of the United States vary from complete livestock grazing to almost pure crop production with only a few animals grazed on crop residues and seed pastures. The larger ranches depend on range forage for the principal part of their livestock feed, but the year-long operation generally involves a combination of range, pasture, and harvested crops for producing feeder livestock. Millions of animals are shipped to the farm states for fattening.

In the mountainous West, cattle are grazed on high-altitude summer ranges for three to five months, pastured during spring and fall, and fed during the winter. On ranches not dependent on national forest or other public lands for part of the yearly grazing cycle, cattle may remain at home on grass range throughout the year. Hereford cattle predominate on the western range. Marketed animals include cull cows, grass-fat steers, and long-yearlings that are generally sold as feeders.

Good practices on cattle ranges demand proper utilization of forage—usually from 30 to 50 per cent of the seasonal herbage production—to permit some grass to go to seed and to allow plant material to fall to the ground to build up soil and form a cover that reduces erosion. Proper utilization can be attained by grazing conservative numbers of animals, by distribution of animals through fencing, salting, and herding to obtain even use of the forage over the range; and by deferred-rotation grazing where portions of the range require nonuse at certain periods in the life cycles of grasses and of other range plants.

Sheep are pastured in many eastern states and in the Northwest on the Pacific side of the Cascade Mountains. In the range country they are grazed throughout the year. Long-distance trailing is necessary to obtain winter forage on the deserts, spring-fall forage in the foothills, and summer forage in the mountains. Lambs are born in the spring and generally marketed in late summer or early fall. The basic breed is Rambouillet. Good practices on sheep ranges require open herding to prevent trampling of the soil and local overuse of forage, rotation grazing and deferment, avoidance of poisonous plants, and frequent moving of herders' camps to avoid use of sheep bedgrounds night after night.

Management in Action

The Forest Service, Bureau of Land Management, and Indian Service manage most of the public grazing lands. Smaller areas are administered by the states, counties, and municipalities. In general, the goal is to conserve the range resource under wise use, but the methods and final results are different.

Any citizen can apply for a permit to graze the public ranges. Preference is given to individuals whose privately owned land can best be used in conjunction with public land. Other qualifications, including ability to care for livestock on the home ranch, amount of livelihood received from ranching, and balance in the ranching program, are considered in determining issuance of range permits. Fees are charged for grazing in accordance with average livestock prices. Grazing on public lands is done under various regulations that concern the term of permit, number, and class of animals, provision for proper management, construction of physical improvements on the range, consideration of wildlife and other uses, range surveys, and cooperation between stockmen and administrators. Livestock boards, composed of stockmen, conduct much of the business pertaining to grazing permits and regulations of the Bureau of Land Management. Forest officers make the decisions for national forest grazing, with advisory boards serving only to express the stockmen's viewpoints.

On Indian Service lands, permission to graze is granted by tribal councils or by families. Leases to outsiders are granted through competitive bidding. State-owned lands are generally leased to private operators, and little control is exercised over use of the land. Restrictions on the use of brands, running of bulls on open range, and inspection for disease vary from state to state. Lands that have reverted to counties through tax delinquency are usually leased to the highest bidder without restriction as to grazing use. Most municipal lands are carefully controlled for watershed protection.

Individual operators on private lands still are very much a law unto themselves. They are subject to few regulations, and they must deal individually with all the complexities of nature. They must be their own botanists, animal husbandmen, watershed managers, soil experts, breeding authorities, economists, and marketing specialists.

Most of them want to do a good job of range management for their own personal benefit. But the majority of them think of production in terms of animal numbers instead of grass, which is the ultimate product they have for sale. And few are motivated by the desire to balance their immediate grazing interests against the wants of hunters, fishermen, recreationists, lumbermen, or the even more remote needs of irrigationists and urban populations for usable water. Hence there is a great need for research, extension, and education programs designed for the practical purpose of helping managers of range and livestock to apply proper grassland standards of use.

The Future

Grasslands are one of our greatest resources, and their proper management is one of our best hopes of survival. The average American is not sufficiently aware that the impacts of increasing industrial development, urbanization, population increases, dam construction, road building, and multiple uses are causing ecological reactions and changes almost faster than we can measure them.

Thirty years ago it was estimated that grazing capacities could be increased 30 to 50 per cent on public lands. Now, that same estimate still applies to the future. In spite of the research that has been done and the guidelines that have been developed, we still are motivated more by the short-term profit desires than by an "ecological conscience." We still have not decided to operate within natural laws instead of disrupting them.

Our greatest need is an early nationwide appraisal of the grassland resource. This appraisal should include not only the land itself, but also the private managers of the land and their managerial abilities, the administrators of public lands and their objectives, and the researchers whose findings are not being fully applied. Such an appraisal should provide a basis for a coordinated national program to insure maximum sustained production from our grasslands.

We need better informed people. The best grassland management, either on public or private lands, will not be achieved until millions of conservation-minded citizens have a better understanding of the ecology of the land. This best grassland management also will not be attained until the people become vocal and insist that administration and research on grasslands be given support commensurate with the value of this great American resource.

If increasing demands for grassland products are to be met, integrated management of public and private rangelands must be achieved. Existing policies and procedures must be revised. There must be cooperation and support of new management programs by all resource users. And the universities, extension agencies, and researchers must do a better job of informing the American people concerning the improvement and management of our grassland and related resources.

For Further Reading

CARHART, ARTHUR H. 1961. *Planning for America's Wildlands.* National Audubon Society, National Parks Association, The Wilderness Society, Wildlife Management Institute. 97 pp.

CLAWSON, MARION, R. B. HELD, and C. H. STODDARD. 1960. *Land for the Future.* The Johns Hopkins Press, Baltimore. 570 pp.

LINDUSKA, JOSEPH P. (ed.). 1964. *Waterfowl Tomorrow.* U.S. Department of the Interior, Washington, D.C. 770 pp.

Outdoor Recreation Resources Review Commission. 1962. *Outdoor Recreation for America.* U.S. Government Printing Office, Washington, D.C. 246 pp.

SAMPSON, A. W. 1952. *Range Management—Principles and Practices.* John Wiley & Sons, Inc., New York. 570 pp.

STEFFERUD, ALFRED (ed.). 1948. *Grass—The Yearbook of Agriculture.* U.S. Department of Agriculture, Washington, D.C. 892 pp.

U.S. Forest Service. 1936. *The Western Range.* Senate Document 199. U.S. Government Printing Office, Washington, D.C. 620 pp.

CHAPTER SIX

FORESTS

Henry Clepper and Lowell Besley

The forests of America comprise five great natural regions.

The Northern Forest, occupying New England, New York, the upper Lake States, and the Appalachian Mountains from Pennsylvania to Georgia, is notable for its pine, spruce, and hemlock, and for its sugar maple, beech, yellow birch, elm, ash, basswood, and red oak.

The Central Hardwood Forest, touching 29 states from Massachusetts to Texas and from the Great Plains eastward, occupies the greater part of the drainage basins of the Ohio and the Mississippi Rivers. It comprises many broadleaf species, with oaks, hickories, black cherry, black walnut, gums, ashes, maples, and yellow-poplar (tulip tree) among some of the more important.

The Southern Forest, occupying the Atlantic and Gulf coastal region and alluvial bottomlands and swamps of 12 states from Virginia to Texas, is best known for its four principal pines—longleaf, shortleaf, loblolly, and slash—although baldcypress, sweetgum, tupelo, yellow-poplar, hickories, magnolias, and other valuable species occur in abundance.

The Rocky Mountain Forest, occupying the high elevations of the Rockies from the Great Plains to the Sierra Nevada, is mostly coniferous, with western white, ponderosa, and lodgepole pines, Douglas-fir, larch, western redcedar, hemlock, Englemann spruce, and true firs. The pinyon pine and juniper of its southern portion are useful for watershed protection—more important than timber in this region.

The Pacific Coast Forest, in California, Oregon, and Washington, contains the world's heaviest stands of timber, including the famous Douglas-fir and coast redwood. Among other species of great value are sugar, western white, and ponderosa pines, western hemlock, larch, firs, cedars, and spruces. Most of the country's remaining volume of old-growth timber is in this region.

In addition, there is a small tropical forest in southeast Texas and southern Florida.

Aside from the inevitable reduction of the original forest area because of the need of cleared land for agriculture, the relatively poor growing condition of much of what remains is the unsatisfactory result of the way Americans have handled their woodland. It is not only understocked (too few trees to utilize all the soil), but it is stocked with a preponderance of trees of the less valuable species or of poor form (crooked, deformed, diseased, or otherwise defective).

Fortunately, the trend of devastation and progressive deterioration resulting from three centuries of wasteful exploitation and inadequate protection from fire and other losses is now being reversed. Timber growth has been steadily rising in recent years as a result of good forestry practices.

The forest area of the United States is 759 million

acres, or one-third of the 2.3 billion acres of land in the 50 states. Of this forest area the U.S. Forest Service classifies two-thirds, 509 million acres, as commercial woodland—that is, land capable of growing continuous crops of industrial forest products. The 250 million acres not useful or available for timber production are nevertheless important for watershed protection, for grazing livestock, for wildlife, and for recreation.

Of the commercial forest land, about 111 million acres, or 22 per cent, are understocked and producing nowhere near their potential; and 35 million acres of this area are too poorly stocked to yield any wood products until they have been reforested. Sound forestry will be necessary to make our timber-producing lands fully productive and to reforest our devastated lands.

The Importance of Forests and Their Products

Forests are one of the world's most valuable renewable natural resources, and wood is one of mankind's most useful raw materials.

Wood products are derived from felled trees. The wood is either used in its natural state or is broken down mechanically and/or chemically into its constituent fibres and other substances. In descending order of volume, the primary wood products are lumber, fuelwood, pulpwood, veneer, logs and bolts, fence posts, ties, mine timbers, cooperage, poles, distillation wood, pilings, and a host of miscellaneous items. With the expansion of the chemical development of cellulose and the improvements in mechanical utilization, the number of wood and wood-derivative products has increased to more than 4,000 items in daily use. In truth, wood in one or more of its myriad chemical or physical forms is indispensable to the production, distribution, and utilization of just about every product—animal, vegetable, or mineral—consumed by civilized people.

Products extracted or harvested from living trees include maple syrup and maple sugar; gum turpentine and rosin; various nuts, berries, and other fruits; holly boughs and other Christmas greens; to mention only a few. Turpentine and rosin are produced from standing trees of longleaf and slash pines; the United States furnishes half the world's needs for these products.

Thus, the forest products industries account for a significant portion of our economic life. According to the U.S. Forest Service (1963), timber-based industries provided employment for 3.3 million people in 1958. The total value added in all timber-based economic activity amounted to $25 billion.

ALLIED PRODUCTS AND SERVICES. Another group of products includes forage, various edible and medicinal plants, economically valuable mosses, and the wild animals that provide aesthetic pleasure and sport to millions of our people.

Forage. Most of the forested lands of the West are a source of forage and shelter for domestic livestock and game animals. About one billion acres of the total land area of the United States are classed as range, and one-third of the range area is forested. Many forest ranges are overstocked and should be rehabilitated by reduction of animals to the range's grazing capacity, by better forest and range management, and by reseeding of worn-out range land. Yet, even in their present condition, they make notable contributions to our beef, veal, mutton, lamb, and game meat and to the hides, skins, wool fat, mohair, and fur we use. For example, in the national forests alone, in 1964 some 19,000 permittees grazed 1.3 million cattle and 2.3 million sheep on the forest ranges in summer. The values of forage, along with the significant relationship of forestry and range management, are discussed in Chapter 5.

Wildlife and Fish. Wildlife and fish are important allied products of forested areas. Publicly owned forests furnish sport for many of the 14 million citizens who buy hunting licenses and the 20 million who buy fishing licenses each year. In the national forests alone in 1965, more than 2 million hunters harvested about 669,000 head of big game—deer, elk, bear, moose, mountain sheep, and goats—while more than one million small-game hunters removed a large crop of grouse, turkeys, hares, and rabbits, and some 20,000 trappers operated their productive traplines. All this recreation is in addition to the vast number of persons who derive their pleasure from observing wild creatures with no thought of killing or capturing them. These forest products are described and assessed in Chapters 7 and 8.

Soil and Water. At the headwaters of rivers and streams, on steep hillsides, and even on gentler slopes where trees occur in hedgerows, shelterbelts, woodlots, or larger tracts, our forests help to hold soil in place and to regulate the flow of water. By intercepting the rain drops with their crowns and trunks, by providing a porous surface of leaf litter and humus, and by holding the soil together with their roots, trees and shrubs retard surface runoff and prevent both sheet erosion and gullying. The

spongy mat and the deep and multitudinous water channel system provided by the tree roots and rootlets greatly
increase the water storage capacity of the soil. Further-
more, cool forest shade retards the rapid spring melting
of the winter snows. In all these ways, the forest helps to
even out and improve the quality of the flow of water
courses and to reduce their siltation.

About one-half of the nation's streamflow comes from
woodland. As much as 90 per cent of the usable water
yield in the West originates on forested watersheds.
Some 75 per cent of the total forest area is critically important for the control of floods and deposit of sediment,
for surface water supply, and for ground water recharge.
Only a small portion of this critical forest watershed is in
a satisfactory condition. The remedy lies in the application of sound forestry measures. Chapter 4 covers the
importance of this subject more fully.

Recreation. Americans find relaxation and re-creation
of body and spirit alike among the trees and rivers, lakes
and mountains, and the wildlife of the forest environment.
Increasing population and tremendous urban growth have
intensified the need for such communion with nature,
while, at the same time, improved transportation and
shorter working hours have provided the means to enjoy
it. Recreational use of the forest has increased to the
point where the impact of people on certain public forested areas and their consequent demands for special
privileges, special services, and special facilities are causing major shifts in the management of both the timber
and allied resources of these properties. Already more
than 134 million visits are made yearly to the national
forests; 121 million to the national parks, and about 292

million to the state forests and parks. This tremendously valuable service of our forests is discussed more fully in Chapter 9.

History of Forest Development and Forestry

From earliest colonial times, Americans drew upon their forests to build a nation. They used logs for homes, fences, and fuel; they used game, berries, and nuts for food. They bartered ship masts, boards, cask staves, potash, tar, pitch, and turpentine for items they could not produce. Long on forest resources and short on workers and implements, they wasted all but the most readily useful parts of the trees cut. In immediate need of agricultural land to feed the growing population, they felled and burned great quantities of prime trees in the clearing process.

Lumbering began its major assault upon our North American forests about a century ago. Vaulting from one billion board feet as of 1840, United States lumber production was 35 billion by 1869, and reached an all-time peak of 46 billion in 1906 and again in 1907. Meanwhile, the center of lumber production moved from Maine to New York (1850), to Pennsylvania (1860), and to the Lake States (1870). Eventually it progressed to the South, and still later to the far West. The myth of the inexhaustibility of our forests, the rush of the federal government to get the land settled, cleared, and developed for agriculture, the enormous demand for new homes, the low prices of lumber because of its great plenty, the developments in rapid lumbering techniques and transportation systems—all contributed to wasteful exploitation, often followed by fires.

The past quarter-century and especially the past decade have witnessed great changes in our industrial forestry outlook. Although lumber continues as our prime user of wood, the phenomenal growth in our pulp and plywood industries is causing major shifts. The pulp industry in particular, because of the high value of its products, its huge investment requiring stable wood supplies, and its ability to utilize wood in small sizes, has had a tremendous influence in reducing waste and in improving the management of our forest lands.

FOREST DEPLETION. Land-clearing for agriculture accounted for the major reduction in the original forest area. Even more important than the cleared or devastated lands is the depletion of the timber resource on the great majority of the remaining forest land still capable of yielding some wood products. Past wasteful logging methods and the enormous losses from wildfire, insects, and diseases have reduced both the quality and quantity of the forest growing stock on much of this land to a point where the forest growth is half or less of the potential of the site. Better management of the forest we have is the greatest need. Obviously the first step is protection.

Fire. Each year in the United States more than 100,000 forest fires burn four to seven million acres. Of every ten fires, nine are the result of human carelessness, human maliciousness (deliberately setting the woods afire), or human indifference. The major offenders are incendiaries, brush-burners, smokers, campers, and railroads.

Wildfire not only destroys standing timber outright or provides conditions favorable for its later destruction by disease, but it is also destructive to the range and to watersheds, it kills game and other wildlife, and it occasionally causes heavy loss of human life. Even light surface fires kill the young trees and small seedlings that make the forest of the future. They burn the leaves and litter on the forest floor, reducing soil fertility. By destroying plant cover on watersheds, fires leave extensive areas subject to erosion. They burn coverts and nests of game animals and birds. Ashes and debris from a fire falling into a stream damage fish habitats. Fire turns green living forests and range lands into blackened wastes—lifeless, desolate, and worthless. Expenditures for the control of forest fires have substantially increased over the years. Federal, state, and private landowners spent approximately $75.5 million in 1965 to control woods fires.

Although wildfire is a great devastator, it should not be confused with the scientific use of carefully controlled burning of surplus slash following forest-cutting operations as a means of reducing the fire hazard in critical areas. Controlled burning is a silvicultural tool often used to prepare the seedbed for the next crop of trees on certain areas where the combination of tree species with climate and site conditions may require it. Such beneficial use of fire must be limited to well-trained and experienced experts. This statement in no way conflicts with that against wildfire, a seriously destructive agent.

Insects. Insects destroy great volumes of timber. In an average year they may kill seven times as much sawtimber as does fire. A single species of bark beetle or defoliating caterpillar may weaken or kill outright the trees on millions of acres. Sometimes the effect of insect damage in a forest is almost as spectacular in its destructiveness as fire. But much damage is of the unspectacular kind, not caused by outbreaks, but by continuous attack seldom seeen or recognized by the public. The total damage by insects is not known, but it is enormous.

Diseases. Trees are susceptible to myriad diseases. Diseases are estimated by the Forest Service to have killed three times as much sawtimber as did fire in recent years. But more than that, the impact of disease on forest growth was twice as great as fire and insects combined. Diseases cause rots, cankers, discolorations to roots, trunk, limbs, bark, buds, and foliage. Heart rots, for example, although greatly injurious, are usually inconspicuous. Other diseases, such as the well-known chestnut blight, sweep through thousands of square miles of timber stands, and kill every susceptible tree. Some diseases, such as chestnut blight and white pine blister rust, are spread by windblown spores. Others such as Dutch elm disease are spread by the contact of insects.

Control of Insects and Diseases. The parasitic fungus that causes chestnut blight has no known cure. Other tree diseases can be eradicated, but usually only at great expense. Likewise, the use of chemical insecticides is sometimes economically feasible, but great care must be exercised to avoid toxic effects upon fish and wildlife. Where possible, foresters, entomologists, and pathologists attempt to control insects and diseases by silvicultural practices.

Since individual insects and diseases usually attack less vigorous trees of a certain species at a certain age in their development, silvicultural methods that produce stands of mixed species, a variety of age classes, and vigorous trees tend to reduce both the hazard of attack and consequent damage. Overmature trees are especially susceptible to disease damage. Partial logging at frequent intervals helps maintain thrifty trees and enables removal of diseased trees or trees of high risk. Development and use of vigorous and resistant planting stock well adapted to the site is another promising silvicultural control method.

RISE OF THE FOREST CONSERVATION MOVEMENT. Forest conservation in the United States became a national movement during the last quarter of the nineteenth century. Previously, nearly everyone thought that fuelwood, logs or lumber for homes and barns, masts, staves, and pitch for export always would be plentiful in America's "inexhaustible" forests.

By 1870, however, thinking people here and there throughout the country began to worry publicly about the nation's reckless handling of the timber resource. The 1,500 people killed and 1.25 million acres burned in the Peshtigo, Wisconsin, forest fire of 1871 shocked many. Others noted the appearance of "ghost towns" in the wake of a lumber industry that always moved on to fresh stands of virgin timber. Consequently, a few newspapers began to editorialize against forest devastation. In 1872, J. Sterling Morton of Nebraska proposed Arbor Day. The next year Congress passed the well-intentioned but ineffective Timber Culture Act to encourage tree planting. That same year the American Association for the Advancement of Science urged Congress and the several state legislatures to take steps to provide timber cultivation and to preserve forests.

The first citizens' forest conservation association in the New World, The American Forestry Association, was organized in 1875. Similar state forestry associations to disseminate information about conservation and to work for the prevention and control of woods fire were organized in Minnesota (1876), Colorado (1884), and Pennsylvania (1886).

Federal forestry work began with the appointment in 1876 of a special agent to investigate and report on forest conditions. This action resulted in the creation in 1881 of the Department of Agriculture's Division of Forestry, which eventually (1905) became the Forest Service. Meanwhile, the Forest Reserve Act of 1891 authorized the President to proclaim national forest reserves out of public domain lands. By 1905, when the reserves were transferred from the Department of the Interior to the Department of Agriculture for administration by the Forest Service, they contained 56 million acres, and by 1907, when they were first designated as national forests, President Theodore Roosevelt had doubled their area to 122 million acres.

State forestry work began with the creation of the California State Board of Forestry in 1885, followed in the same year by Colorado, Ohio, and New York. Prior to 1900, eleven states had thus laid foundations for the protection and management of their woodlands.

The professional status of forestry was recognized by the establishment of the Society of American Foresters in 1900—only two years after the beginning of professional forestry education in the United States in 1898.

Other important highlights in the development of forest conservation, listed chronologically, include:

1882. First American Forestry Congress, Cincinnati, Ohio.

1897. Department of the Interior authorized to administer forest reserves.

1908. President Theodore Roosevelt held White House Conference of Governors on our natural resources; resulted in publication (1909) of first comprehensive inventory by National Conservation Commission.

1911. Weeks Law provided for federal purchase of private forest lands necessary to protect flow of navigable streams (thus began national forests in the East), and began program of federal-state cooperation in protection against fire.

1924. Clarke-McNary Act extended federal land purchase policy of Weeks Act (1911) to include lands necessary for timber production within watersheds of navigable streams; extended federal-state-private cooperation in fire protection and set up cooperation in production and distribution of forest planting stock and in farm forestry extension; provided for study of forest taxation.

1928. McSweeney-McNary Act authorized a broad program of forest research by the Forest Service and a continuing, nationwide, on-the-ground survey of forest resources.

1933. Senate Copeland Report presented the Forest Service's "A National Plan for American Forestry."

1937. Norris-Doxey Cooperative Farm Forestry Act increased technical forestry assistance to farmers.

1947. Forest Pest Control Act provided for federal responsibility in the control of forest insects and diseases and federal-state-private owner cooperation in combatting outbreaks.

1960. Public Law 86-517, the Multiple-Use Sustained Yield Act, declared that the national forests in the Department of Agriculture were to be managed for multiple use and sustained yield of the products and services.

1962. Public Law 87-788, the McIntire-Stennis Act, authorized increased cooperative forestry research at state-supported universities under the administration of the State Cooperative Research Service in the Department of Agriculture.

1963. Public Law 88-29 gave Congressional authorization to the Bureau of Outdoor Recreation created during the previous year by the Secretary of the Interior.

1964. Public Law 88-577, known as the Wilderness Act, created the National Wilderness Preservation System.

1965. The report *Timber Trends in the United States*, issued by the U.S. Forest Service, gave a favorable appraisal of the nation's timber situation.

DEVELOPMENT OF FORESTRY. By 1900 there was a militant, nationwide forest conservation movement, but as yet no true profession of forestry. But forestry was soon to evolve as both a science and an art.

Professional Education. It was early recognized that professional education would be required to train men competent to manage our forests properly. Two schools began offering technical forestry instruction in 1898: Biltmore Forest School in North Carolina and Cornell University in New York. By 1966 there were 43 colleges and universities in the United States offering professional instruction in forestry. Of these, 30 had been accredited by the Council of the Society of American Foresters. Since the first American degree was awarded in 1900, the forestry schools of the nation have granted (through June 1965) more than 37,800 bachelor's degrees, approximately 7,000 master's degrees, and some 1,000 doctor's degrees.

Research in Forestry. Pioneer American foresters were handicapped in practicing their profession by lack of knowledge of the silviculture of native trees. The impressive scientific literature of Europe was only partially applicable to American species. However, the foundation for forestry research had been laid by early botanists and horticulturists and by the studies of the old Division of Forestry.

In 1908, the Forest Service formulated a plan for a system of forest experiment stations, and in 1915 it set up a Branch of Research. In 1928, research received a permanent charter when the McSweeney-McNary Law authorized a comprehensive research program, largely under the Forest Service. It included a system of forest and range experiment stations, more studies of forest products, and a national survey of timber resources. Currently, the Forest Service operates nine regional forest experiment stations and the internationally known Forest Products Laboratory at Madison, Wisconsin. The studies of the experiment stations are further decentralized in one hundred branch stations and research centers.

Research was an adjunct of professional forestry education almost from the establishment of the first school of forestry. Most of the colleges and universities that have schools of forestry conduct research in the production and management, as well as the utilization, of forest crops. Moreover, some state forestry departments early undertook field studies in silviculture, particularly the growing and planting of forest trees. A few states have built laboratories for studies in wood technology and forest products utilization.

Industry research in forestry was practically nonexistent until the 1920's. Then a few large pulp and paper companies, lumber companies, and trade associations set up laboratories and other research programs. From these humble beginnings grew the present considerable industry research effort, largely concerned with products and their utilization.

The total national expenditure by all agencies for forestry and related research in 1965 was about $135 million.

Modern Concepts and Action

FORESTRY IS PROFITABLE. At the beginning of World War II, it was believed that wood, because of its assumed abundance, would serve as a ready substitute for the more critical metals and other commodities needed for war materiel and munitions. However, wood quickly became critically important in its own right when enormous quantities were urgently needed for barracks, cantonments, plants and housing for war workers, ships, aircraft, truck bodies, weapons, and explosives. At one period, half the nation's entire production of lumber and lumber products was used for shipping containers. Actually, the armed forces used a greater tonnage of wood than of steel. Wood is indispensable in the national defense.

With increasing scarcity and increased cost of stumpage (the value of timber as it stands uncut in the woods); with the application of research findings in growing, harvesting, and manufacturing; and with broadening demand for wood pulp, plywood, plastics, fibreboard, and other new as well as old products, the industry is already beginning to make more efficient use of the forest crop. Waste is still enormous in both woods and mill over much of the country. One-fourth of the timber cut is not utilized. But product diversification and manufacturing integration in some of the larger units of the forest industries are leading the way toward more nearly complete utilization of the wood that reaches the mill.

The ever increasing demand for a wider range of wood products contributes immeasurably to the nation's economic welfare. This demand also enables the forest manager to make further use of the timber at his disposal, and to speed up his improvement of the forest growing stock.

FORESTRY REQUIRES COOPERATION. Today it is recognized that the forest owner, whether government or private, and the forest industries, large and small, must work together to make and keep our forests productive. Protection of state and private lands from fire has been a cooperative federal-state-private activity ever since the Weeks Law of 1911. This pattern was expanded under the Clarke-McNary Act of 1924 to cover production and distribution of trees for planting, and farm forestry extension work. Further federal-state cooperation to provide direct on-the-ground technical assistance to farm woodland owners was authorized by the Norris-Doxey Act of 1937, and such assistance has been extended to nonfarm owners and processors of primary forest products by the cooperative Forest Management Act of 1950. Likewise, under the Forest Pest Control Act of 1947, the Department of Agriculture cooperates with the states and private landowners in the control of destructive insects and diseases. Some of the states, and both individual private companies and industry groups, have contributed substantially to the nationwide Forest Survey being continuously conducted by the U.S. Forest Service, and to the report *Timber Trends in the United States*, issued in 1965.

INDUSTRY AND FORESTRY. With less than 10 per cent of our privately owned commerical forests remaining in old-growth timber, the forest industries already are, and from now on will continue to be, dependent upon second growth and subsequent crops of timber for their raw material suppies. Consequently, it is to their interest to assure that supply through the application of good forest management to their own constantly increasing holdings. In addition, they must help other forest landowners grow timber products for future use. For example, the pulp and paper industry employs possibly 5,000 professional foresters to manage its own 35 million acres, from which it obtains about a fifth of the pulpwood it uses, and to give on-the-ground technical forestry assistance to other landowners, who comprise the industry's present and future pulpwood supply.

In addition to the activities of individual companies, the forest industries, through their own national education organization, American Forest Products Industries, Inc. (AFPI), through their numerous trade associations, and through their support of other organizations, are contributing substantially to public education. AFPI certifies as tree farms tracts of privately owned forest land that are protected from fire and managed for continuing crops of wood. In 1966 more than 29,000 tree farms comprising nearly 67 million acres had been certified under this program. AFPI also sponsors the national "Keep Green" program to promote forest fire prevention.

LAND OWNERSHIP AND FOREST PRACTICES. Final responsibility for the wise management of our forest lands lies with the owners, whoever they may be.

Of the 509 million acres of commercial forest land in

the United States and coastal Alaska, the federal government owns 113 million acres (96 million acres in national forests). States, counties, and municipalities own 28 million acres. The remaining 367 million acres (three-quarters of the total) are held by 4.5 million private owners, of whom about 70 per cent are farm owners. With few exceptions, the best-managed lands are those in public and in large and medium-sized private ownerships.

Farm woodlands and those in the small-ownership class are the most poorly managed. In short, the main problem of getting better forest management lies with these two groups that control more than half of the country's commercial timber stands, stands that should supply forest products needed in our economy.

RESPONSIBILITIES AND POLICIES. With this background on current problems, we can better understand the program ahead. The federal lands need better management of the forest resource for their maximum contributions both in primary and secondary products—timber, water, forage, recreation, wildlife—as well as for soil protection. The federal government assists state and private landowners in the prevention and control of forest fires, insects, and diseases; in reforestation where it is needed; and in technical assistance to owners of small forest tracts. In addition, the federal government assists others in carrying on forest and wood research, and public information and education programs.

The state governments are primarily responsible for the management of state-owned forest land, for administration of statewide protection systems, and for providing tree-planting stock for reforestation of private lands. Through education (supplemented by laws and regulations where needed), information, and technical assistance where practicable, the states encourage good forest management on private lands. Also, through state universities and other suitable organizations, some states are carrying on valuable forest and wood research.

Private forest landowners have the responsibility of managing their own forest lands for maximum productiveness and for maximum protection of their own and neighboring lands. Where they are also consumers of timber products from others, they have a special interest in encouraging their wood suppliers to practice good forestry also. And all owners have a stake in protection and education.

A Program for American Forestry

Spearheaded by The American Forestry Association, but formulated cooperatively by leaders in all fields of natural resources with full discussion at the Fifth American Forest Congress, 1963, the new Program for American Forestry provides the framework for a national forestry policy. Its goal is the continued maximum sustained contribution from forest and related lands to the American economy and to the health and spiritual well-being of all citizens.

First, the program recognizes that the protection of forest, range, and watershed lands against damage by destructive agencies is basic to long-range management. Strengthening forest disease and insect research, and state and federal laws and regulatory controls, is recommended. Intensification of fire prevention activity by federal, state, and private agencies and further improvement in fire fighting efficiency are called for.

A basic policy is that the maximum benefits to the economy and to society can be realized if forest and related lands are administered under a multiple-use concept of management. However, the assignment of some areas to special or exclusive use, such as national parks and wildlife refuges, is justifiable within the framework of the multiple-use concept. The reforestation of denuded areas and of forest lands only partially stocked with trees is specially urgent.

For the conservation and improvement of water supplies, the program strongly urges more intensive research in land management to increase water yields. All water users, public and private, should be required to minimize pollution. Cooperative planning for river basin development is also to be further encouraged.

To meet rising demand for outdoor recreation, the federal government, the states, and other political subdivisions need to act now to provide adequate recreational opportunities in woodlands and associated water areas.

Better utilization of wildlife and the improvement of wildlife habitat need to be given higher priority under the multiple-use concept. Likewise, the improvement of range lands through research, and particularly the revegetation of rundown ranges, is necessary for sustained range productivity.

Public, educational, and industrial organizations must expand research in all phases of land management, particularly in problems dealing with timber, watershed, wildlife, range, and the use of these resources for recreation. High priority must be given to the needs of protection, including the prevention and control of disease, insect, fire, and animal damage. Along with improved research is a pressing need for periodic surveys and appraisals, both national and regional, of resource conditions.

More technical assistance to private forest owners, who hold three-quarters of the nation's commercial timber land, is needed to improve the management of these lands and the yield of products and services from them. Incentives, such as financial credit, insurance against loss, and, where necessary, adjustments in property tax laws, should be available.

Constant improvement in resource education is essential to the job ahead. First, it is recommended that facilities for professional education in forestry at the university level be strengthened, a continuing activity of the Society of American Foresters. Secondly, there is need for planned expansion in subprofessional instruction in forestry for the training of forest technicians.

In addition to these two advances in educational opportunity, needs also exist for more vocational training for students who seek instruction at non-university institutions such as vocational high schools or junior colleges. Also, there is an inadequately filled need for education of forest landowners and harvesters to stimulate timber production. Finally, educational programs for the general public are needed to inform people about the conservation of forest and related renewable resources.

To clarify the status and management responsibility of forest and related lands, the Fifth American Forest Congress recommended that studies of land ownership be undertaken in each state. It urged also that a comprehensive review of the public land laws of the United States be made to determine revisions necessary for their efficient management.

Improvements in the harvesting and use of wood are desirable for continuous timber production up to the sustained-yield capacity of the resource. Developing new uses of wood, together with making advances in manufacturing and marketing, is vital to the efficient utilization of forests.

Finally, there is the goal of world forestry improvement. In order that the forest resource, wherever it occurs, may help improve standards of living for people everywhere, the government has been urged to increase its participation in United Nations' activities in forestry and conservation. Such increased participation is helpful in improving educational facilities for professional foresters and forest technicians. Additionally, the widespread exchange of scientific information, through the exchange of forestry scientists, and through more cooperation between conservation associations, will help guide advances in legislation and in national forestry policies.

To sum up: Recent studies by the Forest Service (*Timber Trends in the United States,* 1965) and by Resources for the Future, Inc. (*Resources for America's Future,* 1963), project a continuing and increasing demand for forest products.

Under good forestry management the nation's commercial woodlands have the capability of producing considerably more than they are now producing. In short, if all the forest land were put under the kind of management that the better managed properties get, the expected timber growth would more than meet the projected demands by the year 2000.

Hence, technical forestry practices need to be strengthened to increase future supplies of timber in line with projected demands.

Timber stand improvement, a cultural operation that

includes thinning and removing inferior trees, needs to be applied to millions of acres of young-growth forest.

Planting or seeding of productive sites is another forestry practice that needs to be applied more widely. More than 100 million acres of commerical forest land are now poorly stocked with good quality trees. In contrast, during recent years the area of land planted to trees has been about 1.3 million acres.

Increased protection from fire, insects, and disease will produce higher wood yields. Mortality losses have been greatly reduced in recent years, but they still amount to the equivalent of one-third of the net timber growth.

Expanded work in research and development is essential to provide the knowledge for more efficient management of the forest resources and improved technology in the wood-using industries.

In conclusion, we as a people must realize that forests are one of the most valuable natural resources in our nation. We know that this is true when we consider the extent and distribution of our woodlands, the numerous useful articles they produce, the valuable services they provide, and the industries and communities they support. The more efficiently our forests are managed, the more abundantly they can be made to yield the timber, water, wildlife, forage, and recreation that our expanding population needs, now and in the future.

For Further Reading

ALLEN, SHIRLEY W., and GRANT W. SHARPE. 1961. *An Introduction to American Forestry*. McGraw-Hill Book Co., New York. 3d ed. 413 pp.
American Forestry Association. 1963. *A Conservation Program*

for American Forestry. The American Forestry Association, Washington, D.C. 32 pp.

CLEPPER, HENRY (ed.). 1963. *Careers in Conservation.* The Ronald Press Co., New York. 112 pp.

—— (ed.). 1966. *Origins of American Conservation.* The Ronald Press Co., New York. 193 pp.

——, and ARTHUR B. MEYER. 1965. *The World of the Forest.* D. C. Heath & Co., Boston. 128 pp.

DANA, SAMUEL TRASK. 1956. *Forest and Range Policy: Its Development in the United States.* McGraw-Hill Book Co., New York. 1956. 453 pp.

FROME, MICHAEL. 1962. *Whose Woods These Are: The Story of the National Forests.* Doubleday & Co., Inc., Garden City, N.Y. 360 pp.

MEYER, ARTHUR B. 1965. *Forestry as a Profession.* Society of American Foresters, Washington, D.C. 16 pp.

SHIRLEY, HARDY L. 1964. *Forestry and Its Career Opportunities.* McGraw-Hill Book Co., New York. 2d ed. 454 pp.

SMITH, GUY H. 1965. *Conservation of Natural Resources.* John Wiley & Sons, Inc., New York. 3d ed. 533 pp.

U.S. Forest Service. 1958. *Timber Resources for America's Future.* U.S. Government Printing Office, Washington, D.C. 713 pp.

U.S. Forest Service. 1965. *Highlights in the History of Forest Conservation.* U.S. Government Printing Office, Washington, D.C. 30 pp.

U.S. Forest Service. 1965. *Timber Trends in the United States.* U.S. Government Printing Office, Washington, D.C. 235 pp.

Few persons today, however, question that America must have been a striking El Dorado of animal life. In the forested areas of the East were deer, bear, elk, and even buffalo. There were wild turkeys and grouse and passenger pigeons and woodcock. Along the river courses and streams were ducks and geese, raccoons, beaver, otter, mink. In the timbered north woods, wolves, foxes, fishers, martens, wolverines, and lynxes ranged. Westward, across the vast plains and prairies, roamed great herds of buffalo and pronghorn antelope. There were many coyotes, jack rabbits, badgers, and several kinds of grouse. Further west, in the mountains, wandered grizzly bears, mountain lions, wild sheep and goats, and in the skies could be seen such birds as the California condor.

In many instances, the wild creatures, such as the mountain lion and the wolf, had extensive continental ranges, being distributed far to the north and south and from coast to coast. Some, too, were present in unbelievable numbers. Biologists have estimated there may have been 60 million buffalo, 1 million moose, 10 million elk, 2 million wolves, 400 million beaver, 40 million antelope, and billions of passenger pigeons!

On the other hand, wildlife was not everywhere as abundant as some early reports would have us believe. It is understood now, for instance, that the spectacular flights of passenger pigeons and waterfowl created false impressions of other wildlife, making early estimates of unlimited numbers and kinds of animals often erroneous. The unbroken and mature forests of eastern North America did not support really large numbers of big game, like deer, although the burned-over, broken-up forests, whether brought into being by fires from the aborigines or otherwise, probably did.

Present Conditions

What are the changes that have occurred in our wild-life? What is the general picture three and a half centuries after Jamestown?

Anyone attempting to appraise the wildlife situation today from a standpoint of numbers and range must necessarily be cautious, knowing how erroneous were the early reports of explorers and colonists. There is much that is known because of science, and yet, much remains to be learned. Unlike soil and trees, wildlife is difficult to appraise. Fleet, furtive, and often nocturnal, the very nature of wild animals makes calculation of numbers and movements and reactions difficult. This much we do know: that among the extinct species are the over-caught sea mink; the Labrador duck; the passenger pigeon, whose numbers in migration once darkened the sun; the heath hen, which made its last stand on the Massachusetts island of Martha's Vineyard; and the ivory-billed woodpecker, whose habitat in southern forests was destroyed by axe and fire. The California condor, Everglade kite, whooping crane, Eskimo curlew, greater sandhill crane, Attwater's prairie chicken, key deer, and some of the fur-bearers have been brought to the threshold of extinction. The buffalo, after a very close call, is now back to around 25,000 animals (6,300 in the United States), mostly in preserves, parks, and zoos. The elk has been saved in 25 states, and with restocking and good management is considered huntable game now in 11 states. A recent elk inventory shows approximately 300,000 animals in the United States. The moose is down to around 100,000 mostly in Canada and Alaska, with fewer than 11,000 reported in the United States, although the range of the moose has not been constricted too much.

Other hoofed mammals such as mountain sheep, goat, caribou, and musk oxen are fewer in number. So are the big carnivores such as the brown bear, lynx, wolf, mountain lion, and wolverine. In contrast, the black bear is holding its own in the wilder forested areas with some 140,000 reported recently in the United States alone. On the increase, too, are the beaver and a number of the long-haired furbearers such as the skunk, fox, opossum, and raccoon.

The wild turkey is down to 28 per cent of its former range in the United States and Canada, but restocking and good management have brought surprisingly large populations to Pennsylvania, the southeastern coastal and Gulf states, Colorado, New Mexico, and Arizona. The various grouse, particularly the western forms, are reduced alarmingly, but timber cutting has favored the grouse in many northeastern areas.

Where some game species have dwindled, others, notably a few nonnative species, have been introduced and have taken hold and flourished. The Chinese ring-necked pheasant of the northern half of the United States and irrigated valleys of the West is a classic example of a successful species introduction. There has been success on a smaller scale with the chukar partridge, the Hungarian partridge, and the European wild boar.

Waterfowl have notably decreased in number. The destruction of habitat—largely through drainage—and such factors as early market hunting and overshooting led to a steady decline. Ducks hit a serious depression in 1937, then recovered and climbed to a fairly safe population in 1944. Since that time there have been periods of minor decline and upswing with somewhat stable continental populations continuing. Two species of ducks, the canvasback and the redhead, have shown marked decline, while the wood duck has shown some slight increases.

Our present wildlife picture would not be complete without a brief mention of the increase of the antelope and deer. Both are present in such numbers today as to afford good hunting on an extensive scale. Recent inventories show the following approximate populations in the United States: pronghorn antelope 273,000; white-tailed deer 4,500,000; mule deer 2,600,000; and black-tailed deer 965,000. Extensive restocking, protection, and the natural fact that forage ranges were in the right stage of vegetative growth have been the chief reasons for this phenomenal increase.

The Value of Wildlife

Wildlife is a valuable resource and serves man in many ways. In early days it contributed greatly to the growth and economy of the continent. The search for valuable peltries, like the beaver and mink, motivated much of the exploration of the New World. The buffalo, slaughtered in great numbers for meat and hides, fed more than 300,000 Plains Indians. The passenger pigeon was easy food for thousands of people. Many of our birds were once exploited for their valuable plumage and eggs, while others, such as quail and waterfowl, were hunted for the market.

The fact that most wildlife is no longer bought and sold does not mean that it now has no value. In a complex, highly organized society like ours, the need for wholesome recreation is understandable. Hunting and fishing provide healthy exercise and body relaxation for millions. According to a survey made in 1966 at the request of the U.S. Fish and Wildlife Service, $4 billion is spent each year by some 33 million hunters and fishermen. This is testimony of the importance of wildlife to our citizens. The half-billion-dollar fur business and the meat value of game also add materially to America's economy.

While the monetary value of sport and recreation associated with wildlife is important in itself, of far greater value are the multiple social benefits gained by wildlife association. Such values in terms of greater mental and physical well-being, while not measurable, are very real; these may, indeed, be the most important values. "Man cannot live by bread alone." He must also live by the spirit. Having dominion over most living things, he must himself somehow aspire to higher social development or cease to progress. That wild creatures have a great capacity for effusing beauty, inspiration, and a certain tonic of wildness is clearly evident in some of our most outstanding works of art, music, and poetry.

Wildlife, too, is important for the role it plays in the biological web of life. Like all forms of animal life, our higher wild vertebrates occupy an important niche in the intricate relationships of living things. It has been evident, for instance, that when certain predatory mammals and birds are killed or driven from an area, there soon occurs an unusual abundance of injurious pests, such as rats and mice. Many animals help to plant and distribute seeds and nuts. Although birds do not always prevent or control insect outbreaks, they are animals of high metabolism and, as voracious feeders, consume great quantities of injurious insects. Birds, too, distribute seeds and act as weed seed destroyers.

History

One of the great incentives that led to the building of America was the exploitation of its bountiful natural resources. High in importance among these resources was wildlife. In the new continent, man could hunt and fish as he pleased. Game was abundant and belonged to everyone. Wildlife, heretofore having known destruction only at the hands of the Indian, and this largely for food, now was more rapidly reduced by new implements of exploitation: the pioneer's rifle, the axe, fire, and the plow. The trapper, with new and better traps, pushed deeper and deeper into the wilderness after peltries.

That wildlife was still abundant a century and a half after Jamestown is borne out by such writings as *The Wilderness Road,* in which the author, Robert L. Kincaid, tells of Dr. Thomas Walker's explorations into western Virginia to locate 800,000 acres of land for settlement. Walker's party of six horsemen spent about five months traveling over what is now southwestern Virginia and eastern Kentucky, during which time they killed 13 buffalo, 8 elk, 53 bears, 20 deer, 4 geese, 150 wild turkeys, and much small game. After his trip, Walker said, "We might have killed three times as much meat if we had wanted it."

During the first two or three centuries after the New World's discovery, the wildlife of North America changed little. Even in Audubon's time, in 1850, few if any birds or mammals were in danger of extinction, in spite of the rise in human population in the United States to 23 million. Then came the "terrible sixty years" of slaughter and decimation and disaster. Buffalo were exploited for their hides and tongues; waterfowl were shot for the market; eggs of wild birds were objects of trade; and bright-plumed birds were shot for the millinery trade. By 1950, in a period of only 100 years, the human population had spiraled to 150 million, a sixfold increase in a century, and had taken a tragic toll of wildlife. For some species, the death knell had sounded.

Most dramatic of wildlife disappearances was that of the passenger pigeon. Schorger says that there were perhaps as many as 5 billion passenger pigeons in America at the time of Columbus. Now there are none. The last single specimen died in the Cincinnati zoo in 1914. In mounted silence it rests in a show case in the Smithsonian Institution in Washington, D. C.

All told, in less than 300 years the white man in America completely extirpated 5 species of mammals and 15 species and subspecies of birds. He has brought close to oblivion 24 more species of mammals and 33 species of American birds.

CAUSES OF DEPLETION.   Although the extinction of an organism is a natural process, the sudden and dramatic disappearance of wild creatures that has taken place in recent times is largely man-caused. Of the many contributing causes of depletion, the two most important are the removal of proper environment—the destruction of forests, wetlands, and grasslands by the pressures of civilization—and the direct decimation of the species itself by overshooting, overtrapping, and poisoning.

The buffalo declined because of overshooting and the

wide destruction of its range, the beaver because of over-trapping, and the grizzly bear (nearly extinct) because of overhunting. Species like the heath hen and the ivory-billed woodpecker fell by the wayside largely because of a man-disturbed environment. What caused the passenger pigeon to disappear so suddenly, no one knows for sure. All causes are speculative. Surely, however, such things as the destruction of extensive forests, commercialization on breeding grounds and the breaking up of great nestings were contributing factors, and came about largely because of man's influence. Excessive shooting was, of course, another important factor.

In more recent years a greatly disturbing new and subtle danger has come to threaten wildlife—pesticides. The widespread use of chemical compounds, notably of the hydrocarbon group, has caused serious concern among wildlife biologists. Evidence is strong that some threatened species, like the American bald eagle and certain other birds of prey, are, through food chains, directly affected by the use of certain pesticides.

EARLY LAWS AND ORIGIN OF CONSERVATION PROGRAMS. While our forefathers took wildlife for granted and looked upon fish and game as a matter of course, a few champions of conservation began lifting their voices in protest even in colonial times. Earlier bird protection dealt mostly with game birds, but it is significant that this led to eventual protection of nearly all species. One of the first states to enact a law for wildlife was New York, in 1791. The Commonwealth of Massachusetts in 1818 forbade "the wanton destruction of useful and profitable species." The passage of state game laws followed closely on the heels of the retreating frontier, reaching California and the Pacific in 1852. By 1880, all the existing states had game laws in some form or other.

In 1885, the Bureau of Biological Survey was organized in the U.S. Department of Agriculture, resulting from the interest of such men as Dr. C. Hart Merriam, its first chief, and Dr. A. K. Fisher, and a group of ornithologists who had started what is now the American Ornithologists' Union. The new bureau was given the mission of aiding farmers in protecting their crops from animal and bird depredations.

In 1891, Wisconsin took steps to give ducks a measure of protection. In 1894, Yellowstone National Park was closed to public hunting. In 1900, Congress passed the Lacey Act, which prohibited the importation and interstate shipment of any wild bird or mammal, or part thereof, that had been taken or possessed in violation of the laws of any state or foreign country. This excellent law finally gave the federal government supervision over interstate commerce in illegally taken game.

In 1903, President Theodore Roosevelt, in sympathy with the recommendation of the Audubon Societies and because he was himself a wildlife enthusiast, began setting aside by executive order areas of government-owned land known as "Federal Bird Reservations," with the understanding that for a time at least the Audubon groups should bear some of the expenses of guarding them. The first national wildlife sanctuary, Pelican Island in Florida, came into being, setting a precedent for the establishment of a great number of federal and state refuges.

The National Association of Audubon Societies (now the National Audubon Society) was organized in 1905. The first attempt to give federal protection to migratory birds came in 1904 with the introduction of the Shiras bill. It failed of passage, and not until 1913 did the Weeks-McLean Law give the government control over migratory birds. This control was strengthened with the passage of the Migratory Bird Treaty Act and conclusion of the Migratory Bird Treaty with Canada in 1916, and a similar treaty with Mexico in 1937.

WILDLIFE MANAGEMENT BECOMES A SCIENCE. The development of the science of game or wildlife management came on the heels of the early 1930's. The late Aldo Leopold, often referred to as the father of wildlife management, wrote his famous book, *Game Management* (1933), setting forth in theory and principle the ways of managing wild game for recreational use. It was a scholarly and comprehensive presentation, and led the way for the development of courses in wildlife management at many colleges and universities.

Simultaneously with this intensive educational training in wildlife, a movement got under way for intensive research in wildlife. Research centers, known as cooperative wildlife research units, were established at 18 colleges, and the much needed work of game research and the training of wildlife workers began in earnest. Today wildlife management is an established and widely recognized profession.

Modern Concepts and Practices

The control over wildlife as we know it now in America stems from the legal codes of England, where the Magna Carta provided that the King owned all game and distributed it to his subjects as a personal prerogative. When the colonists arrived in the New World, a new concept of wildlife ownership came into being. Depending on game for food, the colonists judged that hunting and fishing were free to all the people. The individual states later took over the ownership of game, including its protection, and ruled that the individual citizen became owner only after he reduced it to possession in a legal manner. The principle of state ownership and control of wildlife has been maintained to this day and has but one major exception—the control of migratory species by the federal government—and in a few minor exceptions, where states have ceded the wildlife on certain lands to the federal government.

Modern concepts and practices in the management of wildlife stem from several sources, chiefly trial and error and the findings of wildlife science. We know now, for instance, that the artificial propagation of game for restocking wild environments is largely a waste of time and money. The idea came into popularity in the 1920's and 1930's, when it was assumed that pen-raised birds were the means to assure game abundance. Game farms sprang up around the country and the hand-rearing of certain species began on a large scale. The impracticability of this idea soon became apparent, however, and game farms shortly began to go out of business. Experience demonstrated that the restocking of hand-reared game in areas where native stock was present, but not doing well, was futile. If the better, stronger, native wild stock could not effect an increase, pen-reared, half-wild animals, new to a strange environment, could not be expected to do so. A few states still maintain game farms, but only because of public demand stemming from groups unaware of the pertinent facts. Today the game farm is a tool of game management to be used only when justified, such as perhaps raising brood stock for release in areas where no parent stock exists, or for release ahead of the gun under artificial hunting conditions where the shooters pay the cost. Live-trapped wild stock is preferred by the modern game manager when restocking seems advisable.

State after state has gone out of the hatchery business and, in turn, has trained its sights on such basic measures as providing a suitable habitat for wildlife, adequate protection, and good management. Game animals are looked upon as products of land use to be grown as harvestable crops like corn or hay. It is recognized that wild creatures will multiply and thrive only to the extent that food, proper habitat, and protection are provided. Food is basic and must be present in the right amount and in the right quality each day of the year. Cover is likewise a fundamental need of all wildlife. Without some place to hide from enemies, including man, to find shelter from the elements, and to den or nest and rear its young, wildlife cannot survive.

Since wildlife is a product of our land and water areas, and this to varying degrees, depending on suitability, it is clear that how we manage these areas will largely determine how many wild creatures will exist. Land will produce grass and crops, trees and livestock. Likewise, it will produce quail and rabbits, songbirds, muskrats and wood ducks. Depending on man's wishes and activities, the land can be made to produce one or more or all of these products in varying amounts. This concept of multiple land-use—that is, of getting the greatest and best productivity out of each acre—is not new, since instances of good land management have been known for many years in Europe. The emphasis now placed in this country on multiple use and its companion, sustained yield (continuous yield without danger to the supply), is fairly recent, however.

With the recognition of the need for soil conservation in America and the commendable work of the U.S. Soil Conservation Service, the classification of lands according to best use has come into prominence. Lands are now adjudged according to their most effective productive use and are classified and mapped. Wildlife is given a place in the land pattern, although not necessarily always the major place. On the other hand, the idea that land unsuitable for anything else is good for wildlife is a dangerous concept and might well be discarded. Poor land is poor in productivity of all crops, wildlife included, while good land—the most productive land—is usually the most productive of all crops, including wildlife.

The problem that arises, of course, is what is most important. Is it food or recreation? Is it beef cattle or quail? Is it oil or waterfowl, sawlogs or wild turkeys? The interests are not always incompatible, although some serious problems have arisen in assigning wildlife its rightful place in the land pattern. These are being resolved as foresters, land managers, and biologists work out conflicts in the public interest as they see it.

A matter on which thinking has changed in recent years is that of regulations and law enforcement. Once directed toward a policy of inviolate preservation, game laws today are tools of management aimed to restrict, increase, or distribute the legal take to the safe allowable annual surplus. The expansion of some forms of wildlife, such as deer and elk, into agricultural areas makes it essential that controls be combined with protection. This has resulted in management by "species," with groups such as big game, small game, furbearers, and waterfowl receiving highly specialized treatment.

Proper harvest, too, is a new concept. We now know, for example, that undercropping can be as bad as overcropping. In some game species, quail for instance, it has been found that the safe harvest is half the fall population. If the hunter does not take this surplus, nature will. Correspondingly, with deer, where the range's carrying capacity is fully utilized, it is necessary to crop the population by a number equal to the increment; otherwise the deer will exhaust the supply of accessible browse, and invite disease and starvation. Cropping the bucks, does, and fawns alike is the only way to keep the herd in balance. Certainly, the application of the "buck law" has no place where animals have reached the carrying capacity of their ranges.

Another concept that is being viewed in a different light is the matter of predation. A subject of controversy even today, predator control, once thought to be the magical formula for more game, has lost many of its adherents and has been relegated to the status of a practice useful in extreme or local areas. At best it is simply another tool of management.

Management in Action

Wildlife conservation is now a big enterprise in America. Management programs in varying degrees are in action in all parts of the United States, Canada, and Mexico. Most of the activity has to do with the manipulation of many kinds of environment and is concerned with many occupations, involving agriculture, forestry, and grasslands and wetlands management. It often deals with the expansion or restraint of both animal numbers and human activities.

Managing wildlife at the federal level in the United States is the responsibility of several agencies, the principal of which is the Bureau of Sport Fisheries and Wildlife, a part of the Fish and Wildlife Service of the Department of the Interior. Under its broad scope come such activities as law enforcement, inventories of waterfowl and other game, predator control, the management of wildlife—particularly ducks and geese on its 238 migratory waterfowl refuges—the protection of endangered species, and research in various areas of wildlife science.

Wildlife conservation was given impetus several decades ago with the passage of two major pieces of legislation by Congress: the Migratory Bird Hunting Stamp Act of 1934, and the Federal Aid in Wildlife Restoration Act of 1937, usually known as the Pittman-Robertson Act. The former, resulting from the reckless destruction of ducks and geese for the markets and of other birds for their plumage and eggs, provided for a special license for hunters wishing to take waterfowl. The proceeds go toward the purchase of badly needed federal bird refuges. The refuge program, under the leadership of J. N. Darling, chief of the Biological Survey in 1934 and 1935, was actively promoted during this period. With the help of the Civilian Conservation Corps, the Works Progress Administration, and other "emergency" programs, a great system of federal wildlife refuges was built up.

The Pittman-Robertson Act has often been referred to as "the best thing that has happened to wildlife." Funds derived from an 11 per cent federal excise tax on guns and ammunition are allocated to the states on a matching basis

(75 per cent federal funds, 25 per cent matching state funds), going toward approved projects aimed at restoring and improving living conditions for game birds and animals. As an example, during the fiscal year 1964, P-R funds helped finance 736 wildlife restoration projects, on which the 75 per cent federal share of the costs totaled $19,482,383. The various projects in federal aid include research, land acquisition, construction and development of wildlife areas, and the maintenance of completed work.

In the area of waterfowl conservation, management by the Fish and Wildlife Service, in cooperation with the states and the Canadian provinces, has two major objectives: (1) the enactment of hunting regulations geared to the increment, and (2) the bringing of additional wetlands and water areas under management. Here modern census techniques applied on the northern breeding grounds are providing valuable data for use in setting seasons and bag limits. On federal and state waterfowl refuges, intensive work is going on in water-level control and the growing of marsh plants for food.

Besides the Fish and Wildlife Service, other federal agencies in close cooperation with the states are active in wildlife management work. The U.S. Forest Service, through its Division of Wildlife Management, and with its great system of 151 national forests totaling 181 million acres, is doing commendable work managing wild game and conserving threatened species, such as the California condor and the Kirtland's warbler, through protective measures and habitat improvement. It has been estimated that one out of every four deer killed annually in the United States is taken within a national forest. Because of the size and importance of federal forest areas in the states and the fact that the states have jurisdiction over game, the matter of interagency cooperation is often complicated. Over the years, however, enabling legislation by many of the states and cooperative agreements have ironed out initial conflicts, and now excellent progress in game restoration and management is being made. Present-day cooperation between the states and the U.S. Forest Service on areas like the two national forests in Virginia, where model forestry and game practices are under way, testifies to the degree of understanding that now exists between governmental agencies on federal lands.

In similar fashion, a great deal of management work is being done in many of the major river basins of the country where the federal government has taken over vast public areas. Staff biologists of the Fish and Wildlife Service and the state fish and game departments work closely with the Corps of Engineers and the Bureau of Reclamation in outlining and promoting programs favorable to wildlife and in the best public interest in accordance with the provisions of Public Law 732, the Wildlife Coordination Act of 1946.

Not to be overlooked, too, are the activities of such agencies as the Soil Conservation Service and the soil conservation districts organized in every state, the Bureau of Land Management, the Bureau of Indian Affairs, and the important National Park Service with its 32 national parks (13,619,099 acres) and other public reservations. All are engaged in the protection and management of wildlife in one form or another.

Great impetus to the use of wild lands for recreational purposes and wildlife conservation was given by the 1962 report of the Outdoor Recreation Resources Review Commission. This led to the creation of the federal Bureau of Outdoor Recreation in the Department of the Interior. Subsequent action by Congress has provided funds (through the Land and Water Conservation Fund Act) for the acquisition of lands and the development of recreation and wildlife programs at the federal, state, and local levels. A major advance for wildlife preservation in undisturbed, roadless areas, characterized by natural, primitive conditions, took place with the passage in 1964 of the Wilderness Act.

On the states' part, the work of management is done by conservation departments or fish and game commissions, chiefly supported by hunting and fishing license revenues and federal-aid funds. Besides administering the game laws of the states, these agencies have programs of their own aimed at long-range wildlife conservation. Some are better than others, depending upon the agency setup and the leadership. All have programs of habitat improvement, and are working closely with landowners and other land-use agencies, such as the Soil Conservation Service, in attempting to give wildlife a better home. Many states, like Pennsylvania, have extensive land-purchase programs, in the belief that public lands are the only safeguard to some semblance of public shooting in the future. Others are acquiring rights-of-way and access areas to existing public hunting areas, and many are simply buying and setting aside wetlands and other wildlife areas for the day when future management will be possible.

The state fish and game departments, of course, differ in their policies and methods of administration. Some are still politically controlled; others are fairly free of political pressure. One-man rule has given way in most states to the commission type of policy-making body. Administrative and field workers are acquiring more technical training. Good departments with well-rounded programs usually exhibit the following structural characteristics: Freedom from pressures, political and otherwise; a merit system and adequate salaries for personnel; consistency and stability of policy; close coordination among all resource agencies concerned with land use; and a sound program for conservation education.

Interest in wildlife conservation is not restricted to government agencies. A score of conservation organizations are also fighting for the well-being of wildlife. Meritorious work has been and is being done by the Izaak Walton League of America, nationally and through its local chapters; the National Audubon Society and its many branches and affiliates; Ducks Unlimited, with its fine waterfowl restoration work in Canada; and the National Wildlife Federation with its many state affiliates, to mention only a few. The work of the Wildlife Management Institute in supporting research and education work in wildlife and in promoting the annual North American Wildlife and Natural Resources Conferences is worthy of special mention. So is the commendable work of The Wildlife Society and its professional wildlife biologists; the International Association of Game, Fish and Conservation Commissioners; the various regional associations of fish and game officials; flyway councils; the American Association of Conservation Information; and the Conservation Education Association.

The Outlook

What lies ahead for American wildlife? For the wildlife conservationist, at least, one thing is certain: His problems loom large and grave. Such problems as the continued loss of habitat, water pollution, the continued use of dangerous pesticides, rising hunting pressure, a multiplicity of encroachments on wildlife areas, crop damage, and other conflicts of interest will be his to resolve. All of them are actually aspects of a larger basic problem, which is how to reconcile an ever upswinging human population and its attendant ever increasing demands on wild creatures with a constantly shrinking habitat for wildlife. This poses serious questions for both the game administrator and the biologist.

In America, the pioneer days of hunting, fishing, and trapping for food are long past. Yet a lively interest in and concern for wild creatures remains. The vast sums of money spent annually by those interested in hunting and fishing and in the aesthetic enjoyment of nature indicate, rather paradoxically, a strong desire for the continued existence of wildlife. This is good, for wildlife is essential to man's well-being. More leisure hours gained through a shorter work week will mean more outdoor recreational pursuits, more spending of money for licenses, equipment, and travel, and more expenditures by game agencies for conservation efforts.

Although man can do much to increase the productivity of some forms of wildlife, such as deer, antelope, and wild turkey, and may be successful in introducing a few more exotics, like the ring-necked pheasant, the clear fact remains that there is a limit beyond which wildlife cannot increase. As the human population rises, man will have to take less and less wildlife. We shall have to appreciate wildlife more—or lose it. To keep it, we must somehow extract more hours of recreation from each form that is taken or pursued. The emphasis will have to be away from *kill* and *meat* to *let live, share,* and *enjoy.* To enjoy wildlife more, we shall have to give further encouragement to such less destructive activities as bow-and-arrow hunting, wildlife photography, bird watching, and aesthetic enjoyment. Personal discipline and ethics will have to be raised and standards of sportsmanship greatly elevated. More attention will have to be focused on the higher forms of activity associated with wildlife and less on those of the consumptive levels.

Evidence clearly points toward temporary stopgaps to counter the combination of mounting gun pressure and less game. Already there are signs, distasteful though they are to many, that the hunter is willing to accept a high degree of artificiality in his sport. The releasing of hand-reared game on private shooting preserves is strongly before us. The leasing of hunting rights by small groups and clubs willing to pay a higher price for their sport is now common practice. These trends are bound to continue.

To meet hunter demands, the various conservation agencies will resort more and more to species management and to the closer utilization of harvestable surpluses. The multiple use of ranges and forests on public lands will be intensified. Federal and state game agencies will be drawn even closer together in their management activities. The nongame forms, and especially the threatened species, will receive increased attention.

To insure some place for the average citizen to hunt or otherwise enjoy wildlife, the states no doubt will continue to buy and lease land for public use as wildlife recreational areas. While there can never be a sufficient number of these to insure good hunting for everyone, the feeling is that these areas will allow limited controlled use, and may prove one answer to the demand for token public hunting in the future. Especially is this true for some big-game species such as deer and antelope and for the smaller forest game. Such public areas, too, along with an increasingly enlarged system of other public lands, will serve the added purpose of assuring a continued breeding stock from which restorations can be made.

In the matter of farm game and waterfowl, the annual take will necessarily have to be geared to the annual crop of harvestable animals. This will mean tighter restrictions on public lands. Where the gun pressure gets too great, the permit system of regulating hunter numbers will be used. On private lands, the fee system now growing in vogue will be intensified. On private lands adjoining intensively managed public lands, the device of wildlife damage insurance undoubtedly will be resorted to on a larger scale.

Man has learned much in recent years about the mechanics of producing game for recreational use. This knowledge will grow and be useful. Science, too, will uncover new and better ways of producing more game. But the problems ahead are largely those of managing man's activities, not game. Obviously the time has come when man himself must be managed and geared to an available wildlife supply. This will take more special education and better public relations. Some states, seeing this necessity, are providing for such programs by the initiation and the intensification of conservation education programs. Already such highly effective tools as nature centers in urbanized areas, outdoor laboratories, and school and college "land-for-learning" areas are coming into vogue. Many states also see the need for sound wildlife policies and efficient administration and will strive to attain those ends. They see the promise of other states moving ahead where there is little political interference. The trend among the states, slow but sure, is toward a representative body of commissioners for policymaking and for career men in wildlife science to carry out those policies.

If we are to maintain some degree of naturalness about us, we must accept new attitudes, new philosophies, new outlooks and habits of life. The old ways will not do. Now we know "that there is a point where independence becomes irresponsibility and liberty becomes license." The modern conservation ethic stipulates that since our life-sustaining natural assets belong to all and are enjoyed by all, all must share in the responsibility for their safekeeping and intelligent use.

When man's activities are so managed that they will not be detrimental to a continued wildlife supply, when he has learned to temper his demands and share nature's benefits, then the future of our wildlife will be assured. This can be accomplished. The obstacles are not insurmountable. Whether it will be accomplished is another matter. The decision rests in the wisdom of the American people, the quality of leadership of its resource managers, and the ability of us all to accept and put into practice a new and enduring philosophy of life based upon the concept of wise resource use without abuse.

For Further Reading

ALLEN, DURWARD L. 1962. *Our Wildlife Legacy.* Funk & Wagnalls, New York. Rev. ed. 422 pp.

BLACK, JOHN D. 1954. *Biological Conservation—With Particular Emphasis on Wildlife.* McGraw-Hill Book Co., New York. 328 pp.

Camp, Raymond R. 1948. *The Hunter's Encyclopedia.* Stackpole & Heck, Inc., Harrisburg, Pa. 1,152 pp.

Day, Albert M. 1959. *North American Waterfowl.* Stackpole & Heck, Inc., Harrisburg, Pa. 329 pp.

Gabrielson, Ira N. 1959. *Wildlife Conservation.* The Macmillan Co., New York. 2d ed. 244 pp.

Graham, Edward H. 1947. *The Land and Wildlife.* Oxford University Press, Inc., New York. 232 pp.

Kaufman, Erle. 1956. *The Conservation Yearbook.* Monumental Printing Co., Baltimore. 320 pp.

Leopold, Aldo. 1933. *Game Management.* Charles Scribner's Sons, New York. 481 pp.

Mid-Century Conferences on Resources for the Future. 1953. *The Nation Looks at its Resources.* Resources for the Future, Inc., Washington, D.C. 418 pp.

Seton, Ernest Thompson. 1953. *Lives of Game Animals.* Charles T. Branford Co., Boston. 4 vols.

Stoddard, Herbert L. 1946. *The Bobwhite Quail.* Charles Scribner's Sons, New York. 559 pp.

Trefethen, James B. 1964. *Wildlife Management and Conservation.* D. C. Heath & Co., Boston. 120 pp.

Trippensee, Reuben Edwin. 1948 and 1953. *Wildlife Management.* McGraw-Hill Book Co., New York. Vols. I and II; 479 and 572 pp., respectively.

Wing, Leonard W. 1951. *Practice of Wildlife Conservation.* John Wiley & Sons, Inc., New York. 412 pp.

CHAPTER EIGHT

FISH

Albert S. Hazzard and William Voigt, Jr.

Fish was a basic food for the American Indian. Fresh, or smoked and dried, it was a staple for his family and his dogs. The early settlers, too, found a large and seemingly inexhaustible supply of fish almost everywhere. Along the coasts were great numbers of marine species—cod, flounders, weakfish, sea bass, and many other fine fishes. Shellfish, crabs, and lobsters further varied the diet of the pioneer. During the spawning runs, the rivers teemed with salmon, shad, and other species that ascend rivers from the sea in order to breed.

Interior waters also abounded with fish. Eastern brook trout ranged the cooler waters west to the Mississippi, and in the West the rainbow trout and the many related forms of the cutthroat mingled with the Pacific salmons to form an unparalleled fishery. The vast Mississippi drainage supported the various basses, the walleye, the catfishes, and other valuable food and game species. The Great Lakes supplied the whitefish, lake trout, yellow perch, and other fishes so important to the Indian and to the westward-pushing pioneers. True, the original fauna of some waters was limited to a few species, but their great abundance made up for the lack of variety. Fish, then, supplied one of the principal items in the diet of the early and growing population of North America.

Development of the present economy in the United States has greatly affected the fisheries. Dams for water power early blocked the runs of salmon and shad into the streams of New England and more recently have seriously affected the more important migration of the Pacific salmons and the steelhead.

Pollution from sewage and, more acutely, from industrial wastes has interfered with the passage of young and adult fish from the sea and has limited the habitat suitable for shellfish and other marine forms. Inland waters have also suffered from this scourge. Thousands of miles of otherwise fine fishing water have been taken out of production because of the acid and other drainage from coal mines or the poisonous effluent from industrial plants.

Deforestation and drainage to exploit more land for agriculture, by destroying shade, have warmed streams to the point where they can no longer support trout. Consequent erosion and siltation have further damaged the stream habitat for all the more desirable fishes. Food is smothered, spawning beds are ruined, pools are filled in, and stream channels widened and made shallow. Much fine trout water has also been spoiled in the name of flood control and the protection of highways and bridges.

Overfishing has been another factor, especially for such commercial species as the Pacific halibut and salmons, and for trout in many inland waters. Sound regulations based on research have restored the halibut and the salmon fisheries, and will be used in the future management of commercial fisheries. Scientific management of the sport fisheries is now being developed.

On the positive side of the ledger, the introduction of

new species of fish has increased and varied the yield. The shad and the striped bass have been successfully transferred to the Pacific coast, although attempts to bring the salmon from that area to Atlantic streams have not yet succeeded. The introduction of the brown trout from Europe has created fishing where the native species can no longer survive. Establishing the rainbow trout in the East and the brook trout in the West has further varied the sport fishing, though it perhaps has not increased the total production. The smallmouth bass and the walleye were brought into such river systems as the Potomac, the Delaware, and the Susquehanna, and are now the principal sport species in these streams. Of course, mistakes were made, too. The carp has roiled many formerly clear bass waters since its introduction and dispersal during the latter part of the nineteenth century. Yellow perch have ruined many fine trout lakes instead of benefiting the fishing.

The creation of multipurpose reservoirs, such as those of the Tennessee Valley Authority, and large impoundments in Texas, Oklahoma, Kansas, and the Dakotas have provided fishing where little existed before. The creation of many thousands of farm ponds, especially in the southern states, has tremendously increased the yield of valuable protein food and has resulted in many hours of healthful recreation.

The past 60 years have seen a marked change in public attitude toward sport fishing. Once considered primarily the occupation of the lazy man or the rich dilettante, angling has now become a most respectable recreation. Presidents fish, and leading doctors are advising this gentle sport for the overworked businessman. There has been a marked change, too, in our attitude toward the fish themselves. The pioneer was thinking almost entirely of food when he caught a mess of salmon or trout. Today we consider the sport of fooling an active game fish and bringing it to net as the prime reason for a fishing trip. Indeed, many anglers now release, unharmed, most of the fish they catch on their delicate tackle and artificial lures.

Economic Importance of the Resource

Inevitably, conflicts have developed between sport fishing and commercial fishing. The fight that was brewing in the Great Lakes over these interests in the lake trout has quieted only because of the mutual concern over the depredations of the invading sea lamprey. The salmon everywhere has aroused these conflicting interests, and of late the striped bass along the eastern seaboard has been a point of contention. Happily, some such conflicts can be resolved by the commercial fishermen becoming guides to the sportsmen. It has happened, bringing a larger income at less risk. Frequently research has shown no real competition between these interests, but where it does exist, these authors believe commercial fishing must always yield. More people benefit in every way when fish can be taken for sport.

Although today we are not so dependent upon food from the water as were the early settlers, fish and shellfish still rank high in the American diet. The latest (1963) compilations of the total commercial catch in the United States (including Alaska) show a total of almost 4.8 billion pounds, with a value of some $377 million. Of course, much of the poundage and income is derived from the so-called by-products—fish meal, fish oil, and fertilizer. However, these compilations show a per capita consumption of fish as food of 10.6 pounds per year (much less than, for example, in Japan or in the Scandinavian countries). Some 128,470 fishermen with 11,928 boats of all types harvested these fish. The Gulf states lead the regions of the United States in the total poundage of fish and shellfish harvested, followed closely by the Pacific region. However, in order of value, the two regions are reversed. Menhaden used for fish meal and oil lead in poundage in the Gulf states, with mullet, red snappers, and groupers the principal food fish. Shrimp lead in value of the catch. The tunas and salmons lead in poundage and value in the Pacific region. The Great Lakes and Mississippi fisheries are at the bottom of the list in quantity and value. Man is principally dependent upon the sea for his food fish.

A total of 20,219,457 fishing licenses were sold in the United States from July 1, 1964, to June 30, 1965, but this is only part of the growing army of anglers. In most states persons younger or older than certain age limits are allowed to fish without a license; also, on their own waters, resident landowners, their immediate families, and tenants. Only six states require a license to fish in salt water. The 1965 National Survey of Fishing and Hunting estimates that the total number of sport fishermen (aged 12 and over) in the United States was 28,348,000 in that year. If one estimates that each fisherman took an average of only ten pounds, the total yield was 280 million pounds. Valued at fifty cents per pound, the catch was worth $140 million. Various attempts have been made to assess the economic value of sport fishing aside from the meat value of the yield. The revenue from licenses alone in 1963–1964 was $60,213,427, which may have employed some 16,000 fish culturists, wardens, biologists, clerical, and administrative workers.

Examining the figures from the Survey in the study reported by the U.S. Fish and Wildlife Service in September, 1966, we find that the 28,348,000 Americans who went sport fishing in 1965 spent approximately $2.9 billion in pursuit of their sport.

The recreational value of angling to the participant is intangible and is difficult and perhaps impossible to determine. Is it fair to assume that a fisherman gets as much recreation per trip as from attending a baseball game or a good Broadway show? The National Survey showed that the average angler fishes 18.4 days per year. If we estimate the worth of his recreation at $5 per day, a conservative total value of $2.6 billion results.

Of course the ardent angler will not admit that a day at the baseball park or an evening at a show is the equal of a trip to his favorite stream, lake, or seashore, and many doctors would be inclined to agree with him. The fresh air and the sunshine, the more or less strenuous exercise, and the complete freedom from responsibilities combine to tone the muscles and freshen the spirit. If the fishing can be done away from the crowd and in a beautiful setting, the aesthetic values are further enhanced. Fishing can be a family affair, too. It appeals to both sexes and to all ages. In these days where so many forces tend to separate a family group too early, any recreation that can be shared by all is of special value to society.

Fish and Related Resources

Fish have direct relationships with other natural resources and their exploitation, primarily through their essential environment, the water. Forests cool the flowing streams, conserve precipitation, and release it gradually. The types of soil in the drainage determine the mineral content of the waters and their productivity in fish through an often complicated food chain. For example, waters from limestone areas are more productive than those draining surface soils low in soluble calcium.

The manner in which these basic resources of soil, water, and vegetative cover are utilized also affects fish life. Maintenance and restoration of forest and grasslands on steep slopes or other areas subject to erosion, and proper agricultural practices will help to stabilize streamflow and keep damaging silt out of the waters. Mining and the withdrawal of other basic soil products may affect fish through silt released by washing the coal or other minerals, or by chemical pollution as from acid mine drainage or crude-oil escape.

The way man uses the water itself profoundly affects fish production. Dams block free movement of migratory species and destroy stream environment; however, in some cases the riverflow may be stabilized and the reservoirs created may more than equal the original stream in fish habitat. Drainage for agriculture and diversion of water for human consumption, for power, and for irrigation pose more serious threats to fish life. Saner use of waters to remove domestic and industrial wastes must be developed if their full capacity to produce fish and afford recreation is to be achieved.

Fish must also share the waters with other animals. Predation by turtles, suckers, water birds, and amphibious mammals such as mink, otter, and seals has long disturbed anglers and commercial fishermen. Careful studies of feeding habits and other ecological relationships have shown that, although some predation may lessen fish production locally, the overall effect of these forms on fish is minor and perhaps more beneficial than harmful. Most fishes are extremely prolific—from hundreds to millions of young are produced annually by a single female! The waters can support to maturity only a small fraction of these young. Predators also play a useful role in removing sick and defective fish, and since they do not feed selectively, they may benefit man by preying on useless or competing species. Perhaps more serious competition in trout waters comes from beavers. Although the fur is valuable and the animal and its workings are of interest to the recreation seeker, the damage done to trout is often serious. The dams block spawning runs, kill essential shade, and silt-in pools and food-producing gravel areas that are essential to reproduction. Beaver populations must be carefully controlled on many watersheds if trout fishing is to be maintained.

Early Attempts at Improvement

As has been stated, the development of our present-day civilization over the years has seriously depleted the fishery resource, through pollution, soil erosion, and other forms of habitat impairment, and through overfishing.

Early in the nineteenth century, concern began to be expressed for the declining fisheries. The disappearance of the Atlantic salmon, primarily caused by dams, resulted in demand for protective laws and for fish ladders. Concern was also soon felt for trout and other inland fisheries. Legislatures enacted laws requiring fishways around dams (most of which proved to be ineffective) and established restrictions on the taking of fish. First outlawed were certain types of nets and traps. Next, closed seasons were established, frequently combined with size limits. Late in the nineteenth century, daily creel limits were set. These have been successively lowered through the years. In most cases the restrictions placed on angling have not been based upon known facts, but have been precautionary in nature. Extension of such protection to the pan fish, such as sunfish, bluegills, and perch, was natural, but after intensive scientific investigations had proved the fecundity, abundance, and lack of adequate harvest of these warm-water species, the trend was changed and the laws began to be modified.

Artificial propagation and transfer of fish also developed in the latter part of the nineteenth century. This was believed to be the answer to depletion—plant millions, nay billions of young fish and all would again be well! Introduce new species so that all waters would teem with all kinds of fish.

The United States Fish Commission was established in 1872 to investigate the alleged depletion of fish and to prescribe remedies. Fish commissions were organized in several states shortly thereafter.

Restrictive laws and hatcheries were the keystones in all these attempts to stem depletion. The federal agency, although it began as an investigative body and has always attracted some of the best fishery scientists of each age, early succumbed to the bright promise of fish culture, and soon much of its appropriations and those of the state agencies were used for this purpose. At present all states and territories have fish conservation boards, bureaus, or commissions, usually combined with similar game or wildlife bodies and frequently included in a general natural resources department; all are financed largely or wholly by funds derived from fishing licenses.

The earliest conservation programs were concerned

with the decline of the food fishes—the salmon and shad. Later, shellfish, lobsters, and shrimp were investigated, largely through federal efforts, and conservation programs were developed in the various states having such resources. In some states there are separate bureaus or commissions that deal with the commercial fisheries. They are financed by general funds, but in a few states, as in California, at least in part, by a tax on the fish production.

The Science of Fish Management

The science of fish management has developed slowly until recent years. Early pioneering efforts were largely in England, Scotland, and the Scandinavian countries, and in Germany and France. Discovery, near the start of the twentieth century, that the growth of fish could be determined from the scales has contributed much to the present program. Marking studies, especially to development of tagging, has supplied needed information on migration, population density, and the current rate of exploitation. New instruments and techniques in oceanography (such as underwater photography and automatic recording thermometers) have contributed to better understanding of the fishes' environment. Development of sound regulations and other management techniques through research have been keys to the improvement of fisheries everywhere.

Scientific management of sport fisheries and, to a lesser degree, of commercial fishing was long retarded by preoccupation with fish culture and artificial propagation and planting, but this situation seems to be changing. The federal government was, and still is, largely concerned with improving the yield of food fishes. Until the 1930's, few states carried on much research aimed at scientific management, but, especially since the advent of the federal aid program in 1951, recent progress has been rapid.

Today, a search for new information to apply toward improvement of fishing, together with the application of newly gained facts and sound theories, is a basic part of the natural resource conservation and management program of every state, although the degree of emphasis varies, sometimes greatly, among the states.

Development of the ecological approach, and the devising and refinement of techniques for fishery studies, were stimulated by an awakening public interest, the presence and growth of which were reflected in the burgeoning of local, statewide, and national organizations of sportsmen and conservationists. It is probable that fishery management practices common today could not have been instituted as recently as a decade ago because management knowledge and conviction had not crystallized, and because public understanding and support were lacking or inadequate.

Generally speaking, in the fresh waters that have been kept reasonably free from pollution, modern concepts of fish management are such as to encourage a maximum harvest while seeking only to assure survival of sufficient brood stock to guarantee adequate reproduction. Investigators have discovered, and seemingly proved, that in many cases larger returns to the fisherman can and should be allowed than had been thought feasible in an earlier part of the century. This is particularly true of the so-called warm-water species, which, for the most part, appear to require far less protection from the angler than was previously believed.

Nowadays, the tendency of the progressive fisheries

manager is to take a liberal attitude toward season, size, and creel limit until experience proves him wrong. The ascendancy of this type of thinking and practice could not have come without research, inquiring minds, opportunity to experiment, and widespread dissemination of newly learned facts through modern media of communication.

Nearly everywhere, today, the tendency is toward brevity in and simplification of laws and regulations governing recreational fisheries. This trend is modified and slowed, though not entirely checked, in some areas by reason of special prevailing conditions. As one example, it appears that trout waters will usually support less harvest pressure than waters better suited to the more tolerant and prolific spiny-rayed warm-water species. Hence, liberalization has advanced further and faster in the case of fishing involving the spiny-rayed types. An additional fact, one among many, is that in the northerly and easterly sectors of the country, the trout waters often are affected by large human populations and industrialization, both bringing attendant pollution and a drain upon other resources having a protective or stabilizing relationship to water, such as timber and other vegetation, and soil.

Threats to the Future of Fishing

The future appears to hold a mixture of promise and threat in the fishery field. Promise lies in the ever growing store of new knowledge of fishery conditions, problems, and needs, and in the apparently increasing willingness of administrators and the public to apply the new knowledge. It is found in the better recognition by those concerned for the future of fishing of the threats that hang over it. These threats should not be minimized. They vary from place to place, but are genuine, and great.

In the West, the physical act of bringing irrigation water to fertile areas deficient in rainfall has damaged or destroyed important fisheries, and there is no reason to believe that the program of water diversion for farm purposes will decrease in extent or intensity. Hydroelectric power dams have an irresistible allure to most westerners. More streams, not fewer, will be blocked by dams halting the free passage of migratory species and limiting if not eliminating their numbers. Until or unless recognition of the value of the western fisheries becomes more widespread, and measures are found and applied to counter damaging water management practices, the present trend will not be checked, much less reversed. The claim that the impounding or diverting reservoirs will prove productive enough to compensate for the fishery losses that they cause does not stand up under critical scrutiny except in most unusual exceptions to the rule. Many portions of productive streams have lost their fishery resources because of depleting types of water utilization.

In the eastern half of the nation, which has more rainfall, a present threat is the increasing diversion of surface waters for municipal, industrial, and agricultural use, and the likelihood that new laws to govern and control such usage may not give adequate recognition to fishery values.

And, over all, there hangs the constant menace of pollution. Despite the genuine progress being made, there is much evidence to show that as a nation we are barely holding our own in the control of water pollution. The realist sees what is happening and cries out against it, but is often brought up short by the countering reality that an abrupt halt could, and perhaps would, mean just as abrupt a halt in the flow of material things that he has come to regard as necessities of modern living. Even the most complete and efficient modern sewage-disposal plants leave an oxygen-consuming residue to be assimilated by the receiving stream. Industrial waste-treatment facilities likewise leave much to be desired in virtually every case. And the laws and controls far too often either are deficient in themselves or are administered and applied less than perfectly.

Increase in the intensity of existing pollution can result from the additional diversion from streams of water wanted for city water supplies, industrial processes, or irrigation, for, as the cleaner upstream water is removed from the stream bed, the diluting effects of the flow are decreased.

Kinds of Action Needed

There is need for taking inventory of existing water supplies in virtually every state, certainly in all states east of the Rocky Mountains. It should come prior to the enactment of water rights (appropriation) laws in the eastern states; but if it does not, it surely should be a condition plainly stated in the law. Then, with existing supplies of water known, the quantities that may be diverted under law should be based upon minimum flows, rather than average or maximum flows. And in every instance where a perennial stream is affected, the new laws coming to the Middle West, East, and South should specify plainly that no such stream may be depleted by diversion to a point where beneficial aquatic life is endangered.

It seems a certainty that this type of new law is fast

coming to the wetter states east of the Rocky Mountains. Those who respect and value fish and fishing, for food or recreation, must prepare themselves and be ready to contend to the utmost for the minimum guarantees outlined above, if they wish to see a fishery of consequence perpetuated for America. Large impoundments and farm ponds alone will not provide for the public need.

While the new trend in legislation seeks ostensibly to guarantee a fair volume of water for each user, too often the users considered are only those who have a profit-seeking interest. The nonconsumptive recreational use of water is given little attention when the opposing forces are commercial or municipal. Those demanding a fair share for recreational water use are often brushed aside as "standing in the way of progress," and must therefore fight harder to achieve recognition of their demands in the writing of the laws. This condition is likely to intensify rather than diminish in the years to come, unless recognition of the varied benefits of fishing and fishing opportunity comes more rapidly in the future than it has in the past.

As the national population grows, as industrialization increases, and as the demands made upon arable land become more intense, public policy inevitably will be to try to guarantee that material needs are satisfied first. Recreational requirements, the needs of the spirit that may be satisfied so greatly in the outdoors, especially that portion of the outdoors that contains clear, clean water, will continue to be a concern of a minority. Thus vigilance and aggressiveness must be maintained, and the power of sheer numbers countered by ingenuity and intellect.

The alternative is that sport fishing may become the recreation chiefly of the fortunately situated, or the wealthy who can travel long distances to find it. That alternative must not come to pass.

For Further Reading

ALLEN, SHIRLEY W. 1959. *Conserving Natural Resources—Principles and Practice in a Democracy.* McGraw-Hill Book Co., New York. 2d ed. 370 pp.

American Fisheries Society. 1965. North American Fish Policy. *Transactions of the American Fisheries Society,* 94:117–118.

LYLES, CHARLES H. 1965. *Fishery Statistics of the United States, 1963.* Statistical Digest 57, Fish and Wildlife Service. U.S. Government Printing Office, Washington, D.C. 522 pp.

———. 1965. *Fisheries of the United States, 1964.* U.S. Fish and Wildlife Service, Washington, D.C. 71 pp.

WALFORD, LIONEL A. 1947. *Fishery Resources of the United States.* Public Affairs Press, Washington, D.C. 134 pp.

CHAPTER NINE

PARKS AND WILDERNESS

Howard Zahniser and Michael Nadel

America's oldest natural resource is the latest one to be recognized as in need of conservation. It is the wilderness, out of which has indeed been fashioned our civilization, but which itself has been greatly diminished in the process. Now recognized as a resource with distinct values, it is being more and more deeply appreciated, and protected with increasing success. It comprises areas in contrast with those where man and his own works dominate the landscape, areas where the earth and its life community are untrammeled by man, where he himself is a wanderer whose travels leave only trails.

Only a few centuries ago, all of what has since become the United States was wilderness, as indeed, were likewise the lands that are now its territories and possessions. Within this wilderness the aboriginal human inhabitants were themselves so completely members of the continent's life communities that the land, though occupied by them, still stayed wilderness.

Our wilderness now is one of remnants. Even so, it is remarkable that after centuries of mechanized exploitation by a multiplying population, there still are extensive

152

areas unspoiled. Much of what remains is in private ownership, or in such a category that its destiny for development has already been determined. On the other hand, a great deal of wilderness is within areas of publicly owned land where so far it has been preserved, and where it can be preserved indefinitely. It is this part capable of being preserved that constitutes our wilderness resource.

By its constitution, New York State maintains, "forever wild," its great stretches of forest preserve in the Adirondacks and Catskills—2.4 million acres in the former, 240,-000 acres in the latter: a total of some 2.6 million acres. Maine has the historic Mount Katahdin wilderness in its 193,254-acre Baxter State Park. Michigan has a wilderness in its Porcupine Mountains State Park, 57,366 acres in the Upper Peninsula. California has close to .5 million acres in wilderness stretches within a half dozen of its state parks. There also are other states that have some areas still preserving wilderness conditions—South Dakota with Custer State Park, for example, and Minnesota with Itasca State Park.

The largest remnants of wilderness that constitute an important natural resource of the American people, however, are for the most part on some 55 million acres owned or controlled by the federal government. These are within wildlife refuges and game ranges, national forest areas, national parks and monuments excluding, of course, the parts of the parks and monuments taken from the wilderness to provide roads or accommodations for visitors, and on public domain lands. There are remnants of wilderness on Indian reservations if the Indians choose to preserve them.

Out of its total land area of 2.3 billion acres, including Alaska, this nation thus has—in federal and state areas—

a wilderness resource aggregating about 58 million acres or more, hardly more than 2.5 per cent of our total land area.

Parks for Recreation

Containing much of our wilderness resource and also serving purposes closely related to those of wilderness preservation are many and large areas in parks—municipal, county, parish, state, and national. Of all the artifacts of culture that man has fashioned from the wilderness, this institution called "parks" is possibly the most distinctively American, and the one that differs least from its original wilderness raw material. The concepts of the park and of the wilderness as a cultural resource are so closely related that they are commonly associated. Both are also closely related to other uses of the outdoors.

The American people have always in great numbers sought recreation in the outdoors—in the nearby woods and fields as well as in forests, along neighborhood streams and ponds as well as on lakes and other more distant waters. Native wildlife has held interest whether close to home or in distant habitats. In parks and wilderness this interest, this attraction, has simply been most intense. In parks, it has been most attractive to the largest numbers of people and there, except for the actual presence of the people and their accommodations, the wilderness and its resources have been protected from exploitation.

None of the 50 states is now without a state park. In all, some 2,479 state parks include 5,763,142 acres, attracting 284,795,025 visits, according to 1962 statistics.

How many Americans use city, county, and other local parks would indeed be hard to say. In 1961 the National

Recreation Association, in its *Recreation and Park Year-book*, reported a total of 24,710 parks including 1,015,461 acres in 2,221 counties and cities. The park habit is part of the American character.

The greatest of all American park concepts is the national park idea. The essence of its most creative purpose was in the elder Frederick Law Olmsted's explanation of his 1858 plan for New York's Central Park. His son, another Frederick Law Olmsted, more than half a century later wrote the historic phrases in which Congress defined this purpose, "which purpose is to conserve the scenery and the natural and historic objects and the wildlife therein and to provide for the enjoyment of the same in such manner and by such means as will leave them unimpaired for the enjoyment of future generations." This definition was part of the basic Act to Establish a National Park Service approved by President Woodrow Wilson on August 25, 1916, a culmination in the development of a concept that had started half a century earlier but that very recently had been desperately threatened and was certainly in need of reaffirmation.

Fifty years later, the National Park Service administered 232 areas—parks, monuments, and sites of various sorts, but all designated for some degree of preservation in status quo and all for the benefit and enjoyment of the people. More than 121 million visits were recorded in these areas in 1965. The marvels of the national park system and its popularity are statistical as well as aesthetic, and they may be represented in tabular form, as shown in the summary of areas administered by the National Park Service in the table on page 156.

The first national park created as such was Yellowstone National Park. On March 1, 1872, President Ulysses S.

SUMMARY OF AREAS ADMINISTERED BY THE
NATIONAL PARK SERVICE
January 1, 1966

Type of Area	Number	Federal Land (Acres)	Lands Within Exterior Boundaries Not Federally Owned (Acres)	Total Lands Within Exterior Boundaries (Acres)
National parks	32	13,619,099	207,068	13,826,168
National historical parks	10	33,359	6,260	39,619
National monuments	77	8,941,778	121,209	9,062,987
National military parks	11	29,368	2,570	31,938
National memorial park	1	69,000	1,436	70,436
National battlefields	5	2,733	1,496	4,229
National battlefield parks	4	7,163	2,105	9,268
National battlefield sites	3	780	6	786
National historic sites	23	3,089	282	3,371
National memorials	16	5,320	206	5,526
National cemeteries	10	220	0	220
National seashores	6	198,078	122,979	321,057
National parkways	3	106,412	15,132	121,543
National Capital parks	1	34,874	2,255	37,129
White House	1	18	0	18
Recreation areas	11	3,497,403	136,990	3,634,393
Total, national park system	214*	26,548,693	619,994	27,168,688

* Eighteen additional areas have been established, and the lands therefor are being acquired. These areas are classified as follows: 1 national historical park, 4 national monuments, 7 national historic sites, 3 national memorials, 1 national recreation area, 1 national scenic riverway, and 1 national seashore.

Grant approved the law declaring that this great "tract of land lying near the headwaters of the Yellowstone River" should be "dedicated and set apart as a public park or pleasuring-ground for the benefit and enjoyment of the people." The act put the park in the control of the Secretary of the Interior and instructed him to "provide for the preservation, from injury or spoliation, of all timber, mineral deposits, natural curiosities, or wonders within said park, and their retention in their natural condition."

The idea of Yellowstone National Park was a campfire inspiration. An exploring expedition, which had gone into the region to test the tall tales of its wonders, camped one night (September 19, 1870) at one of the beautiful sites still preserved there. Some members of the party were discussing the profits they could make by staking out claims. Then Cornelius Hedges—a Helena, Montana, judge—said, "there ought to be no private ownership of any portion of that region, but . . . the whole of it ought to be set apart as a great national park." This is the idea that Congress adopted in creating Yellowstone National Park. This is the idea of our present great national park system.

Wilderness Preservation

In 1858, Henry David Thoreau told in *The Atlantic Monthly* of an 1853 trip he had taken to the Maine woods, concluding his article ("Chesuncook") with a plea for wilderness preservation:

The kings of England formerly had their forests "to hold the king's game," for sport or food, sometimes destroying villages to create or extend them; and I think that they were impelled by a true instinct. Why should not we, who have renounced the king's authority, have our national preserves, where no villages need be destroyed, in which the bear and panther, and some even of the hunter race, may still exist, and not be "civilized off the face of the earth,"—our forest, not to hold the king's game merely, but to hold and preserve the king himself also, the lord of creation,—not for idle sport or food, but for inspiration and our own true recreation?

As frontiers receded, the thought of wilderness as the scene of "our own true recreation" grew in men's minds. Through the years there grew also the understanding that national parks not only preserved the great spectacles of nature for public enjoyment and safeguarded them from private commercial exploitation, but also kept significantly large areas "in their natural condition."

When this purpose of the parks was challenged in Congress, in 1913—by the proponents of a dam in the Hetch Hetchy valley of Yosemite National Park—and the challengers won, the shocking prospect of national park despoliation so aroused the public that the great basic National Park Act of 1916 was passed. The purpose of preservation "unimpaired" was thus affirmed on the highest authority. Wilderness preservation became a distinctive national-park purpose.

At the same time that the earlier national parks were being established, surveys and studies begun by the young Verplanck Colvin in New York State's Adirondacks, in the 1870's, were leading to the laws and constitutional provisions that before the end of the century had firmly dedicated the Adirondack wilderness to protection by the state "forever wild."

When the National Park Service was established by the 1916 Act (under the leadership of Stephen Mather, who became its first director), there were 14 national parks in the National Park System. There also were 33 national monuments that had been established in accordance with a 1906 law (the Antiquities Act) giving the President such authority. At this time there had been established 153 forest reservations within which were the great wildernesses destined to be set aside for preservation by the U.S. Forest Service. In many national forest areas—Minnesota's canoe country, Colorado's Trapper's Lake, New Mexico's Gila headwaters, for example—foresters had begun to think protectively of the wilderness they saw vanishing. In the Southwest, thought took practical form: The regional forester set aside the Gila Wilderness Area, and thus created a new classification. A new American institution was founded.

In 1921 Aldo Leopold, who had conceived of the Gila Wilderness, published a pioneer paper on "The Wilderness and Its Place in Forest Recreational Policy." In 1925 he wrote a notable article entitled "The Last Stand of the Wilderness." In the February, 1930, issue of *Scientific Monthly*, Robert Marshall had published his own classic paper on "The Problem of the Wilderness."

By the 1930's, a national policy for wilderness preservation in the national forests had emerged. A great wilderness champion and interpreter, Robert Marshall, had achieved his position among the administrators of the U.S. Forest Service. Forester, thinker, writer, explorer, philanthropist, he had learned wilderness in the "forever wild" Adirondacks. He had also seen the great western areas of still living wilderness "melting away like the last snowbank on some south-facing mountainside during a hot afternoon in June." He not only worked within the government bureau that handled most of these areas; he also denounced "the tyrannical ambition of civilization to conquer every niche on the whole earth" and, calling on "spirited people who will fight for the freedom of the wilderness," he joined eagerly with others to organize. Thus, by 1935, there were not only wildernesses within national forests and wilderness-preservation purposes within the national parks; there was also an organization called The Wilderness Society—for no broad public purpose seems to be recognized as a distinct one in America without representation in an organization.

No single organization, however, has encompassed American conservation interest in protecting wilderness. All conservation organizations have taken stands in favor of preserving some of the country as wild and unspoiled. When specific areas have been threatened, there have been united protests from all conservation groups with the cooperation also of garden clubs, women's organizations, labor unions, and other citizen groups, as well as individuals. Protests against spoliation have been especially vigorous when the wilderness threatened has been within an area of the national park system.

Maintaining the wilderness areas is also dependent on respect for their human values as wilderness and, beyond this, on what amounts to a broad land-use zoning program. Elsewhere than in our wilderness reservations we can obtain the timber and mineral and other commodities that we need and shall need. Outside our dedicated wilderness we can find the needed sites for our great dams and reservoirs, build the roads and landing fields for our mechanical travel, find also the places for our outdoor recreation with the conveniences and facilities that we so well contrive—in short, realize all the benefits that we want from a developed country. Within our wilderness areas we shall see preserved the community of life of which we by origin and nature are a part, preserved to as great an extent as possible unmodified by our mechanized civilization.

This is a high ideal, based on a reverence for the life community to which we belong, based on a regard for the health of our own minds and bodies and our esthetic or spiritual natures, and based on a concern for the welfare of generations of the future. It is an ideal shared by many people in many ways. In one way or another it is involved in nearly every regard for the wilderness as such. It is an ideal that is in dual jeopardy—threatened because the areas in which it finds its reality are coveted for other uses; and threatened because those who use and protect it as wilderness are so often and so subtly tempted to modify it as wilderness, and thus destroy the quality that distinguishes it from other outdoor recreation areas. The jeopardy is the deeper because the areas of wilderness that now survive are so limited.

The Outlook

Prospects for continued success in park and wilderness preservation in the face of insistent pressures from commercial and other interests are encouraging, but there is no doubt at all that the pressures will continue. As the conditions that create the pressures develop, the needs for the parks and areas of wilderness will also increase. Already the popularity of parks has been demonstrated and the will to provide for wilderness preservation has been in strong evidence, closely associated with defense of park programs wherever these have been threatened. When the inevitable controversies have come to clear-cut issues, the public's park preservation purposes have prevailed.

In further analyzing the trends and needs in connection with park and wilderness preservation and in charting the probable course of public policy, we may find it helpful to make two basic assumptions.

In the first place, we conclude on the basis of our history so far and our observations of increasing populations and the multiplication of machinery that no places are likely through accident to remain in their natural condition unmodified by man. Only those areas that are deliberately set aside for preservation will be preserved.

The second assumption is closely related to and involved with the first: To secure the desirable ends of park and wilderness preservation, we shall have to use our instruments of government to set aside, and insure respect for, areas that can be preserved. No individual land ownership within our culture can possibly give any assurance of perpetuity in wilderness or park preservation in the presence of commercial and other pressures to use the areas for monetary profit. It is the common interest that all men and women share in the perpetuation of the opportunity for wilderness experience that makes it possible, through public ownership and administration in the public interest, to preserve our natural parks and wildernesses. That can be done only by setting aside specially dedicated areas and protecting them in the public interest.

This principle was at the heart of the controversy of the early 1950's that centered on the proposed Echo Park dam in the Dinosaur National Monument and ended in 1956 when Congress passed the Colorado project act, but only after taking out the Echo Park dam—and putting in a statement declaring, "It is the intention of Congress that no dam or reservoir constructed under the authorization of this Act shall be within any national park or monument." Thus reaffirmed after the challenge of earnest controversy, the integrity of the national park system has become more secure than ever, because it has been more emphatically recognized than ever before that the areas in this system are to be preserved from commodity and commercial use.

Preservation of the parks also requires adequate provision for their proper use and care. Public appropriations to provide the needed facilities and to keep them
in good shape; guidance, and often control, of visitors; and
education in the use and administration of the parks are
important requirements. Our American interest in camp-
ing and picnicking and otherwise enjoying our parks and
outdoor playgrounds with conveniences and with automobile access will require more and more development of
suitable areas for these purposes. Their values to healthy
human beings are so great as to warrant much larger expenditures than at present, and we have been much too
slow in realizing this.

There has developed a skilled and progressive park personnel profession within, and under the influence of, the
National Park Service, and in the many state and local
agencies devoted to administering parks for people. The
public has been prompt to take advantage but slow to appreciate the mounting costs and too slow in sensing a
responsibility to care for the parks. Park experts in developing conveniences for the public have helped to make
these areas popular. They have thus demonstrated the
values of the parks to people and have made protection
easier against almost any threat but overuse and inadequate care. Adequate appropriations of public funds and
with them a wise handling of increasingly numerous visitors are almost certain to be prominent concerns in programs for the future.

But in addition to our needs for these well-developed
park areas, for urban and suburban spaces, and for a
countryside of rural loveliness, there exists the growing
need for wilderness, for areas managed to be left unman-

aged, areas undeveloped by man's mechanical tools and unmodified by his civilization. These are our natural areas of wilderness.

All units of government should preserve the outstanding natural areas that remain in their custody. The excellent wilderness-preservation programs under state auspices—from California's custody of primeval redwoods to New York's protection of Adirondack and Catskill forest preserve—should be continued and extended. Such city areas as those within Washington Park in Portland, Oregon, and such county units as the Cook County Forest Preserve in Illinois should likewise be cherished. There should be more of them. And because so much of our remaining wilderness is under federal ownership or control and because federal protection of these larger areas is so much more likely to prove effective than any other, special efforts should be made to strengthen our national programs.

In the national parks, the pressures for roads and non-wilderness recreational and tourist developments threaten in many places to destroy the primeval back-country wilderness. Wilderness within the national wildlife refuges is in a precarious position because the refuges themselves lack adequate legal protection against pressures for commercial or exploitive encroachments.

Wilderness Act

For several years conservation leaders had in fact been considering ways in which effective wilderness preservation could be secured. Beginning in 1956, proposals in Congress to establish a National Wilderness Preservation System were advanced. These proposals received overwhelming public support. The opposition largely was centered in the commodity interests. After eight years of effort there emerged a Wilderness Act (Public Law 88-577), signed by President Lyndon B. Johnson on September 3, 1964.

In its initial provisions the Wilderness Act was less comprehensive than hoped for, but it is the foundation upon which the opportunity exists to preserve a system of wilderness under federal ownership or control.

Under this Wilderness Act of 1964, the 53 areas within national forests that had been administratively classified as "Wilderness" (100,000 acres or over) or "Wild" (under 100,000 but over 5,000 acres), and the Boundary Waters Canoe Area in Minnesota, became the nucleus of the Wilderness System on the effective date of the Act. These 54 areas total some 9.1 million acres.

The Wilderness Act provides for additions to the Wilderness System. The Secretary of Agriculture is authorized to review within ten years of the enactment of this Act each area in the national forests classified on the effective date of the Act as Primitive, as to its suitability or nonsuitability as wilderness, and report his findings to the President.

The Secretary of the Interior similarly, under the Act, is authorized to "review every roadless area of five thousand contiguous acres or more in the national parks, monuments and other units of the national park system and every such area of, and every roadless island within, the national wildlife refuges and game ranges, under his jurisdiction on the effective date of this Act" and report to the President his recommendation as to the suitability or nonsuitability of each such area or island for preservation as wilderness.

The President is to advise the President of the Senate and the Speaker of the House of Representatives of his recommendations, but his recommendations for designation of wilderness areas become effective only if so provided by an Act of Congress. The President's advice regarding areas reviewed for designation as wilderness is to be given with respect to not less than one-third of the areas and islands by September 3, 1967; not less than two-thirds by September 3, 1971; and the remainder by September 3, 1974.

Encouraging as these provisions are, with a great gain for the nation in the substance of wilderness preservation, the provision for continued applicability of the mining and mineral leasing laws to national forest wilderness areas is regrettable, for a wilderness cannot long remain a wilderness if it is subjected to the disturbances created under mining activities. Discontent with this requirement is assuaged by a provision in the Act that no mining patent within wilderness areas shall issue after December 31, 1983. However, the dangers to wilderness in the interval are real.

We can expect that the 34 Primitive Areas, with their present boundaries, would add 5.5 million acres to the Wilderness System; wilderness units of the national parks and monuments amount potentially to some 21 million acres; and within national wildlife refuges and game ranges, some 20 million acres. Together with the 9.1 million acres included in the Wilderness System at the beginning, there is a potential acreage of 55 million in the system under the Wilderness Act, with respect to national forest areas, and units of the national parks and monuments, and wildlife refuges and game ranges.

Further Prospects

Other opportunities for wilderness preservation exist on federally owned lands. These include areas within the national forests classified as "Limited," as well as portions of the national forests not hitherto designated for wilderness purposes.

The Bureau of Land Management may designate suitable areas for wilderness preservation under the land classification Act of September 19, 1964 (Public Law 88-607), on lands that the Bureau administers.

Other potentialities for designation of suitable areas for wilderness preservation exist on Indian reservations, but, of course, such designations, if made, will be of the choosing on the tribal council of each such reservation. Each such area would be subject to the control and jurisdiction of the tribe. The designation of Indian wilderness areas would not merely add to the wilderness reservoir of the whole nation, but, owned by the Indians, could provide a unique recreation resource that would bring them economic benefits.

The primary threat to the maintenance of wilderness areas lies most, after all, in our slowness to realize that an adequate system of wilderness areas must be set aside and zoned for preservation, and thus protected from all uses that are not consistent with continued preservation of the areas as wilderness. This slowness in realization is in turn due to our tardy sensing of the fact that our need for wilderness is fundamental and general, not incidental and specialized. We work for wilderness preservation not primarily for the right of a minority to have the kind of fun it prefers, but rather to ensure for everyone the perpetuation of areas where human enjoyment and the apprehension of the interrelations of the whole community of life are possible, and to preserve for all the freedom of choosing to know the primeval if they so wish.

When this is understood, we shall be very close to having achieved an enduring program for wilderness preservation. But we must at all times remember that our achievement will never be complete or secure until cooperators in all fields of conservation have worked together so effectively that the wise management of all our resources is ensured. Then we shall have provided outside of our parks and wildernesses for adequate production of the commodities we need and for recreational developments that would threaten the wilderness. We shall then have demonstrated that it is possible to preserve a system of wilderness areas without depriving ourselves of essential commodities or of adequate opportunities for outdoor recreation with conveniences. Consistent thus with our civilization, such a wilderness-preservation program may well be expected to endure in perpetuity.

For Further Reading

BUTCHER, DEVEREAUX. 1956. *Exploring Our National Parks.* Houghton Mifflin Co., Boston. 5th ed. 296 pp.
———. 1963. *Exploring Our National Wildlife Refuges.* Houghton Mifflin Co., Boston. 2d ed. 340 pp.
FRANK, BERNARD. 1955. *Our National Forests.* University of Oklahoma Press, Norman, Okla. 238 pp.
GABRIELSON, IRA N. 1943. *Wildlife Refuges.* The Macmillan Co., New York. 257 pp.
JAMES, HARLEAN. 1939. *Romance of the National Parks.* The Macmillan Co., New York. 240 pp.
MURIE, OLAUS J. "Wild Country as a National Asset," *The Liv-*

ing *Wilderness,* Vol. 18, No. 45, pp. 1–29. The Wilderness Society, Washington, D.C. (Includes bibliographical note.)

Outdoor Recreation Resources Review Commission. 1962. *Wilderness and Recreation—A Report on Resources, Values, and Problems.* Study Report No. 3. The Wildland Research Center, University of California. 352 pp.

STEFFERUD, ALFRED (ed.). 1949. *Trees: The Yearbook of Agriculture.* U.S. Government Printing Office, Washington, D.C. 944 pp. (Includes annotated list of wild and wilderness areas in the national forests.)

TILDEN, FREEMAN. 1951. *The National Parks: What They Mean to You and Me.* Alfred A. Knopf, Inc., New York. 438 pp.

CHAPTER TEN

LAND-USE PRINCIPLES AND NEEDS

Edward H. Graham

The dictionary definition of land is "The solid part of the surface of the earth." One of the first facts of geography is that the surface of the earth is three-fourths water. Essentially terrestrial creatures, we feel the vastness of the oceans and the great water areas of the earth as somehow unreal and forbidding. Even the land, as we come to know more about it, seems less friendly than it might, for half of it is desert, mountain, or polar area—much too dry, cold, or otherwise severe for permanent human habitation. Although much of the other half is adapted to the growth of grass, shrubs, and trees, and man can live there in relative comfort, it is a somber fact that not more than one-tenth of the earth's land surface has the combination of climate, topography, and soil necessary for the production of food.

In considering the natural resources that the land provides, we obviously require more than the usual dictionary definition of land. Land is more than the solid part of the earth's surface. It is more than a geographic area. It is

170

more than real estate. Land, as it has come to have meaning to us today, is a natural resource possessing many tangible and intangible values.

The value of land may be expressed in various terms. The use of land for human habitation may be considered its most practical value. Next to habitation, the production of the essential elements of living is most valuable—food, clothing, and shelter. Other uses of land follow as man and his works become more and more diverse. Land for transport, industry, and recreation now has great value. It is now possible to state principles that express the character and value of land from an ecological point of view.

Principles

LAND EXPRESSES NATURAL FACTORS. *It is a principle of land use that an area of land is an expression of all the various natural factors existing in the area.*

Even in this day and age, land represents the fundamental resource to which other natural resources are related and of which they are a part. We have yet to think of resources as being closely related to each other, but only in that way can we properly evaluate them. The animals of an area do not exist apart from the vegetation. The plants depend upon water and the soil. The soil is related to the vegetation as well as to the topography and geologic history of an area. The climate, in one way or another, influences both soils and living things, interdependently. All these natural factors are interrelated and they interact.

Land varies greatly from place to place, depending

upon conditions. The arctic tundra is sparsely inhabited but supports no agriculture. Deserts with low rainfall and poorly leached mineral soils are traditionally nomadic grazing lands, although they are often profitably cultivated when they can be irrigated. Much of the tropics is best adapted to tree growth. The alluvial lands of the world, replenished regularly by flooding, have supported great civilizations from the beginning of history. The temperate zone woodland areas support much of the world's subsistence farming, while the natural grasslands have become our great granaries. Thus we find that there are broad correlations between portions of the earth and the things that man has been able to do with them. We have taken such broad generalizations for granted, but the relation of man to the place in which he lives is basic, and only in degree does it vary for smaller areas and specific sites.

Some of the earliest civilizations were developed in semiarid areas where, along the flood plains of the great rivers, intensive agriculture was possible. The delta lands of the Nile, Tigris-Euphrates, and Indus Rivers saw the growth and development of great social orders. There man selected the soils that were well watered and richly nourished for raising the crops he required.

Early man was not confined to river deltas, however. The history of England shows us that Neolithic man used forested lands to support him. The contemporaries of the fierce auroch and the great Irish elk, these people with their polished stone implements reached the British Isles about 5000 B.C. Their practice of agriculture, together with their flocks and herds, had such an impact upon the native forest that it never recovered.

During recent centuries, the agricultural demands for

land throughout the world have resulted in use much more intensive than any practiced by earlier peoples. Such recent demands, due largely to a greatly expanded human and domestic animal population, have caused destruction of native vegetation, soil erosion, and disturbance of natural conditions on a scale so unprecedented as to constitute conservation and land-use problems quite new in human history.

LAND POSSESSES PRODUCTION POTENTIAL. *It is a second principle of land use that an area of land possesses a characteristic energy system or production potential.*

Throughout the history of modern man the *amount* of land available has not diminished, at least to any appreciable extent. On the other hand, the *condition* of the land has been greatly modified. Today there is no land that is not used, in the sense of its having some value to man. Even the Antarctic has always had a challenge value, and now provides the setting for an unusual example of international scientific cooperation, where twelve nations are collaborating in physical and biological research. The high mountains possess esthetic value and the great deserts a wilderness worth that cannot be duplicated. Elsewhere the lands of the earth have been cleared, cultivated, lumbered, grazed, or inhabited, some of them for as long as human societies have existed.

It is characteristic of man's history that his societies have become steadily more and more complex, and within recent time this complexity has increased at a geometric rate. While this complexity has given rise to infinite problems in the economic and social phases of community, national, and world organization, its effect upon the land has also been appreciable.

A country like the United States with varied land resources and a relatively sparse population may support a high standard of living without precise attention to land-use principles. A small country like Holland, with a high population per unit of land, can enjoy a high standard of living only as a result of meticulous attention to land management. It is doubtful if some of the desert countries of the Middle East can ever aspire to such heights, although the possession of a coveted resource such as oil may for a time support an economy independent of land resources. Some countries, such as Switzerland, exchange for land products the products of their own invention and industry. It must also be recognized that some peoples live largely on the products of the sea. In fact, the land cannot in its fullest meaning be separated from water and the resources that water makes available. But, in a general sense, it remains axiomatic that people depend upon land, and that there is a relationship between the land and its capacity to support a human population at a particular standard of comfort and leisure.

Each site, therefore, is possessed of inherent characteristics that determine its value to man, in terms of the energy he may convert to his purposes. Although man may increase the productivity of a site, such increase bears a direct relationship to the natural characteristics of the site. Only at great expense can a site of low potential be made to produce abundantly. On the other hand, the energy system of a land area is not static, but may vary from time to time in accordance with cultural practices or as natural influences vary—seasonally, as with variations in temperature; over a period of years, as with rainfall; or geologically, as with climate.

CULTURE IS RELATED TO ENVIRONMENT. *A third principle of land use is that the culture pattern and behavior of a people are related to the natural environment that supports them.*

From the time man first used the land, he must have felt the need to make it produce more abundantly. Improvement of wild plants by selection is so old that the world's major crops have no living progenitors in the wild. Irrigation is ancient, and much primitive agriculture was not possible without drainage. In the interior of New Guinea there is a people still practicing stone-age agriculture who turn under vegetation for green manure and use contour terraces for erosion control. In both the New and Old Worlds, mountain lands were made habitable and capable of supporting large numbers of people by well-developed terrace agriculture, including systems of water manipulation. The Greeks used leguminous crops for "reinvigorating" the soil, and the Romans employed systematic crop rotations. In seventeenth-century England, Jethro Tull's "horse-hoeing husbandry" introduced the age of mechanized farming by his machine drill and system of cultivating throughout the growth of the crop. A century later the Frenchman, Boussingault, introduced the era of agricultural chemistry by his pioneer experiments in plant physiology.

Wherever man has used the land, he has shown an uncanny capacity, undoubtedly the result of repeated trial and error over a long period of time, to learn to use the most productive lands for most intensive use. Such empirical method has been followed to the present day. If we once more look to England, a country where land has been intensively used for a long time and whose land-use history is well known, we find that technologic developments over the centuries have steadily improved land yields and helped to support more and more people.

Today we have the advantage of a great wealth of information from the biological and physical sciences that may be applied to more intelligent use of the land. The practical results of such knowledge are in some instances remarkable. The application of minute quantities of molybdenum to the soil, for example, may be sufficient to triple the yield of alfalfa. The United States is a notable example of a country that has increased its agricultural production. Farm production per man-hour has increased more than 75 per cent in the last decade. Today one hour of farm labor produces more than five times as much food and other crops as it did 40 years ago. In 1940, one farm worker supported ten others; today he provides food and fiber for 33 others. Although our per-acre yields in a few crops are still below those of some countries where intensive hand labor gets more from the land than we do, our yields have increased more than 60 per cent over those of pre-World War II days.

In the face of modern technologic "miracles," the natural limitations of the earth are sometimes questioned, and the claim is made that the powers of modern science will make possible food and human necessities without end. But the nature of the earth and the history of peoples show that the natural environment is always a powerful force in determining what man gets from the land. Both science and environment are tools at our disposal. On one hand, the population of the earth is increasing so rapidly as to simulate an "explosion," as the demographers —scientists who study population statistics—have so graphically disclosed. On the other hand, our knowledge increases at an "explosive" rate also. If it could be charted, it is not at all unlikely that the sum of our knowledge would show a steep upward curve approximating that of population and the demands that we make upon our resources.

It has been rightly said that we live in a cultural environment in which economic, social, and technologic factors are paramount. In human affairs this cannot be denied. The point of this chapter, however, is that such cultural environment is inseparable from, and is based upon, a natural environment. The natural and the cultural are interrelated, and should not be thought of as either antagonistic or separate.

LAND HAS NONCOMMODITY VALUE. *A fourth principle of land use is that an area of land possesses human values in addition to its production potential.*

There are many values of land that do not derive from the capacity of a natural situation to produce commodities. Some of them are utilitarian, others are intangible; all of them are real. Among the utilitarian values of land apart from commodity production is site value. All of the works of man—his dwellings, factories, monuments, water impoundments, roads, airports—are located according to his needs and preferences. There must be land on which to place these works, and various kinds of land possess special values for particular purposes. The site value of land has always been important, but as man has increased in numbers the value of site has correspondingly increased.

It is one of the verities of our time that the needs of man have become greater out of proportion to his sheer increase in numbers. No longer is it sufficient for the land to produce food, clothing, and shelter. It must in addition provide many other things. It must provide cellulose for plastic products unknown only a few years ago. It must yield more space for roads, for we travel more and reach farther for food and other products of the land. Even air transport demands land—a modern airport requires 5,000 acres or more. By 1960 more than 50 million acres, including much good agricultural land, had been absorbed by towns, cities, and industrial developments. This shift in land use is accelerating at a rate that is now approaching two million acres per year.

In some of the countries of Europe the demand for land has reached the point where it can no longer be met. The most difficult land-use problems in such countries as Holland and England often center around the most desirable choice to be made from many alternatives, many times involving conflicts between urban and rural demands. In the United States we now recognize the encroachment of urban developments upon agricultural land as a problem of serious national dimensions. Locally, it has meant the disappearance of valuable farm lands suited to the production of specialized crops, as illustrated by the suburban invasion of orange groves and walnut orchards in California and the usurping of truck-crop soils by a turnpike in New Jersey.

The intangible values of land are of extreme importance. "Man does not live by bread alone." As people have come to work shorter hours and gain longer vacations, the demand for enjoyment of the outdoors has increased. There is today a pressing need for more parks and recreational areas. These may vary from easily reached municipal playgrounds and county parks to state, national, and international areas of unique character.

Wilderness areas are being championed by those who wish to camp, hike, or canoe in wild country far from the distractions of the city or urbanized outdoor recreation. Natural areas are often preserved for purposes other than their recreational value. Wildlife refuges may perpetuate homes for rare or vanishing kinds of wild animals and plants. Some areas are protected for their unusual scientific or scenic interest.

This brings us to consideration of land for its aesthetic value alone. The scenic grandeur of landscape has been one of the important reasons for the establishment of public parks, especially those of national and international character. Another reason has been the preservation of the native vegetation and wild fauna that inhabit the areas. In its potentialities for fulfilling an appreciation of the aesthetic, we find the most delicate and sensitive value that can be ascribed to land.

Needs

From the foregoing consideration of principles, we find that certain needs must be met if we are to make the most reasonable utilization of the land resources available to us. Such needs relate to a thorough and appropriate knowledge of the land, an integrated system of instruction in our schools of higher learning, and the practice of good land use by those who work with and manage the land.

LAND INVENTORY. *There is need for a comprehensive knowledge of our land.* The existing systems of land classification are important and pioneer steps in making the most of the capacity of our land to support us. Based on various environmental factors, systems of land classification have been developed as guides for using land without lowering its productive capacity. Such systems are being improved and made more readily applicable to specific purposes. They serve largely to distinguish kinds of land useful for cultivated crops, pasture, range, woodland, and wildlife. Within each of these major kinds of agricultural use, more detailed separations are needed and have to some extent been developed. For crop lands there are capability units; for range lands, range site and condition classes; for woodlands, tree site indexes. There is a growing need for greater refinement of land classification and other guides to use of land for agricultural crops, whether cultivated, livestock, woodland, or wildlife.

Many countries, including the United States, have within recent decades found it necessary to adopt national legislation that provides for various means of production adjustment when the supply of certain agricultural crops considerably exceeds or falls short of the demand. A proper land classification may well serve as a sound, ecologic evaluation upon which such necessary economic adjustments in agriculture may be made. A land capability inventory adequate for such broad agricultural purposes exists in the United States for approximately 400 million acres. The classification of 100 million acres more could be made adequate with some revision. We need almost half the land in the United States classified according to capability, if we are to have a sound basis for a dynamic, nationwide program of production adjustment, acreage allotments, and major shifts in use for our agricultural lands.

The need for a comprehensive land classification extends beyond our agricultural demands, however. We need to know the suitability of all of our land for all potential uses. If we are to approach the urban-rural conflicts in use, we need land-use guides as points of departure. There is little wisdom in the construction of extensive suburban developments on high-quality agricultural soil, particularly if alternative sites are available. Once covered with brick and concrete, productive land is for all practical purposes never again available for agricultural production. Granting that there are many problems that will not be settled by even the most intimate knowledge of land, any group of town and country people who conscientiously wish to develop their community in reasonable fashion will find an inventory and classification of land to be helpful in the solution of their problems. Industrial plants, airports, military establishments, and highways are often located without regard to the inherent character of the land they occupy, and land with recreation, scenic, or esthetic value is often recklessly disturbed. The time has come when we must give careful attention to the values of all available land areas in relation to what we can best do with them.

INTEGRATED INSTRUCTION. *There is need for an integrated system of resource instruction.* It is often remarked that in conservation a scientist or technician may know his own field very well but seems woefully ignorant of any other. On the other hand, a man who knows a bit about a great many things but not much about anything may be so little wanted that he cannot find satisfactory employment. Yet in the conservation field, the only man more valuable than the specialist is the specialist who also is acquainted with fields related to his own. This man is steadily becoming more valuable. The need for him may well be growing out of our increasing awareness of the ecological nature of the world in which we live. It emerges also from the growing tendency to tackle problems as a team. One kind of knowledge may not be enough to solve a problem. For example, we know by experience that soil erosion problems can be solved only by the coordinated efforts of soil scientists, engineers, agronomists, foresters, biologists, range conservationists, economists, and others. The same is true in other fields of land use. The need for coordinated effort is being recognized by administrators in the conservation field who either employ or consult men trained in spheres of activity other than those for which the administrators have primary responsibility.

One of the ways in which to meet the need for coordination in land-use programs is to train men in coordination. Although this can be done by private and public employers, it can be accomplished far more effectively and economically in a college or university. Frequently, the greatest difficulty in coordination is lack of appreciation of the value and importance of the work of others. This attitude could well be changed in a man's formative years. Progress is, in fact, being made in this regard. Some schools are breaking the departmental barrier, so that an engineer, for instance, can get credit for a course in liberal arts. Land-use seminars are employed where students from several departments relate their efforts to answer a single question. A few attempts have been made to give an advanced degree for a thesis that forms part of a larger work in which each part is an integrated portion of a solution to a common problem. This sort of training and experience is invaluable in preparing a student for the work he is likely to be called upon to do in the conservation world. It should be stimulated and fostered to a degree far beyond what has so far been reached in most institutions of higher learning. This is not to deny the necessity for a thorough basic training in a scientific or specialized discipline, for a man is far more effective in coordinated effort if he speaks with real authority in his chosen field.

GOOD LAND USE. *There is a need for the practice of good land use.* In addition to the need for an understanding of land and its capabilities and for properly trained technical personnel, there remains a need for the actual practice of good land use. Experience and accomplishments in conservation in the United States during the past several decades have served to emphasize the fact that conservation depends primarily upon those who own land and those who work with it and manage it. This is true whether the land is a national park, a large western ranch, a 100-acre cornbelt farm, or a city lot. The values of the park can be perpetuated only if the administering public agency is dedicated to perpetuating them. The rancher is solely responsible for the management of the range and its vegetation upon which his livestock and the success of his ranch enterprise depend. The midwestern farmer will determine, through his normal farm operations, whether the soil and its productivity will be preserved or eroded and depleted. The suburban dweller controls the condition not only of his house, but also of his yard and garden, and upon him alone falls the responsibility of whether his place is maintained in good condition.

All of our laws, inventories, and technical skills, as well as all our normal efforts at research and education, are of little avail in achieving good land use unless they can be brought to bear upon the land itself, and unless they become a part of the knowledge and conviction of those who manage the land. As individuals and as a nation we will achieve conservation only as we come to think and act habitually, almost instinctively, in terms of good land use. When the farmer farms on the contour because it no longer occurs to him that there is any other way to do it, as many of our young farmers now do, then conservation has become a reality. It has then become the right and ethical thing to do; it is part of the mores of our society.

In order to practice good land use, individuals and groups must have the support that derives from legal authority and other assistance available from government. Local, state, and federal governments now provide assistance of various kinds in the management of our land resources—technical, educational, and legislative. Noteworthy steps have been taken toward achieving coordinated land use within recent years. The establishment of conservation districts has permitted landowners and operators to organize themselves into legally constituted groups to receive assistance in undertaking good land use. Through watershed legislation, both federal and state, assistance is now provided beyond that available to individuals, especially in the water-management phases of the total conservation job. Such progress points toward the possibility of ultimately achieving a fully coordinated program of good land use on every parcel of land in the United States, through the initiative and participation of individuals and community groups, with proper assistance from local, state, and national governments.

Conclusion

An area of land expresses all the various natural factors existing in the area, and it possesses a characteristic energy system or production potential. The culture of a people, while admittedly a function of their society, technology, and economic order, is nevertheless intimately related to the natural environment that supports them. Land also has value beyond that for the production of commodities.

There is need for broad kinds of land inventory as approaches to natural resource problems and for coordination on the part of those who design national, state, and local programs of resource management. We need to train those who will work with the land in such a way that each will be able to correlate his efforts productively with those of others with whom he must work. And, finally, good land use becomes a reality through the practice of those who own and manage the land.

For Further Reading

CLAWSON, MARION. 1963. *Land for Americans*. Rand McNally & Co., Chicago. 141 pp.

GRAHAM, EDWARD H. 1944. *Natural Principles of Land Use*. Oxford University Press, New York. 274 pp.

LEOPOLD, ALDO. 1949. *A Sand County Almanac*. Oxford University Press, New York. 226 pp.

MACKAYE, BENTON. 1962. *The New Exploration: A Philosophy of Regional Planning*. University of Illinois Press, Urbana. 243 pp.

MUNZER, MARTHA E. 1964. *Planning Our Town*. Alfred A. Knopf, Inc., New York. 180 pp.

SEARS, PAUL B. 1939. *Life and Environment: The Interrelations of Living Things*. Teachers College, Columbia University, New York. 175 pp.

STAMP, L. DUDLEY. 1955. *Man and the Land.* William Collins Sons & Co., Ltd., London. 272 pp.

U.S. Department of Agriculture Yearbooks: 1955, *Water,* 751 pp.; 1958, *Land,* 605 pp.; 1963, *A Place To Live,* 584 pp. U.S. Government Printing Office, Washington, D.C.

WOOTEN, HUGH H., *et al.* 1962. *Major Uses of Land and Water in the United States, with special reference to agriculture.* U.S. Government Printing Office, Washington, D.C. 54 pp.

CHAPTER ELEVEN

NEEDED:
A NATURAL RESOURCES
POLICY

Ira N. Gabrielson

The development of the movement for conservation of renewable natural resources approached maturity when the fact finally became apparent that it is impossible to manage one resource independently of the others.

Most of the older conservation organizations, in their earlier stages of development, concerned themselves with only one or two resources. One of the most noticeable phenomena in the past three decades has been the growing understanding that it is impossible to develop one segment of renewable resources without impinging directly or indirectly upon others.

There are numerous organizations interested in birds, mammals, fish, plants, grasslands, forests, soils, and water. Many others are devoted primarily to particular phases of land, water, and wildlife management. In water management alone, for example, there are private and official groups interested in hydroelectric power, flood control, irrigation or reclamation, recreation, drainage, navigation, water pollution, and industrial uses. In the agricultural field, the number of organizations is legion.

These diverse organizations approach resource management from as many different angles as there are human viewpoints involved. It is inevitable that there will be some clash between the interests of these groups whenever attempts are made to translate their ideas into action. However, nearly all groups interested in single resources gradually have come to realize that attainment of their own goals depends largely upon the manner in which the other resources are managed. This realization is perhaps the most significant conservation development of our time. It has brought about demands for better correlation in all natural resources programs and stimulated many efforts to develop more comprehensive policies.

Some of the policy statements of recent times are those proposed by the Natural Resources Council of America (see Appendix A) and the land- and water-management policy proposals by the Outdoor Writers' Association of America, the Izaak Walton League, the Chamber of Commerce of the United States, and the American Forestry Association. In 1955 a uniform policy was proposed by the President's Advisory Committee on Water Resources. There have been many others, and these few are mentioned merely to illustrate the widespread efforts in this field. They are examples of the growing interest in developing a coordinated policy of resource management, as well as of a determination on the part of many people that such a broad and comprehensive policy shall be developed.

This demand has been stimulated by the launching of many one-purpose projects that have damaged other resources, and resulted in losses that could have been avoided, or at least minimized, by careful consideration of all inherent resource values before the projects were undertaken. The most widely publicized examples have been with respect to water, where needless destruction of anadromous and unique native fisheries resources has resulted from the building of dams for navigation, flood control, hydroelectric power, or reclamation without proper consideration for biologic resources. Some dams have eliminated flowing streams that supported desirable communities of fish life not found in reservoirs. In other cases, precious forest lands have been unnecessarily flooded, where it might have been possible to develop water-management programs without destruction of forest resources. Waste of that kind is certain to exist when there are several agencies of government engaged in isolated and uncoordinated water-management programs.

Multiple-Use Management

The growing number of conflicts over single-purpose programs has led to the development of broader concepts that frequently have succeeded in correcting some of the more glaring shortcomings in the original plans. As examples of this, the combination of sustained-yield and multiple-use programs for the management of forest lands has made considerable progress, both on public and private lands, and has resulted in retaining more values than could have been retained under the old "cut out and get out" logging practices. The multiple-use concept has been applied more successfully, perhaps, in the management of timber lands than in that of other resources. This is as might be expected, since there really are no great inherent conflicts in the basic uses of most forest land.

There are forest areas that do not lend themselves readily to multiple use, or which are so valuable for one special use that management must give that use precedence over others. There are, however, vast forested areas to which multiple-use management has been applied successfully.

The application of the multiple-use concept to water resources has received much lip service from government agencies concerned with water-management programs. But, because of the size of many of the projects and the traditional background of the various management agencies, there has been, until recently, little real multiple-use thinking in the developing of plans for water use. There is a growing recognition of the fact, however, that water-development projects frequently can produce more value by considering all resources. Even if some programs have to be modified drastically to serve more resource values, such modifications may provide more benefits.

One of the difficult problems in applying the multiple-use concept to water projects is the fact that some uses of water are antagonistic to others. It is difficult to reconcile water storage for flood-control purposes and water storage for hydroelectric power or reclamation purposes. A flood-control impoundment or series of impoundments should be managed to maintain a minimum volume of water in order to store the maximum amount of flood water if optimum flood control is to be attained. Efficient management for hydroelectric or reclamation purposes calls for the storage of as much water as can be held during periods of runoff. The result is that there often is little storage available when unexpected floods come. Reconciliation of these conflicting interests means a sacrifice of efficiency and values in one or both fields. This frequently leads to conflicts in management after the facilities are completed.

The development of coordinated policies has proceeded further in land management than in the field of water management. This can be attributed largely to the efforts of the U.S. Soil Conservation Service, which has developed many sound techniques for the management of land and promoted their widespread application. Perhaps the greatest progress has been due, however, to the development of a mechanism to carry out these programs. The concept of using local associations of landowners in soil conservation districts is practiced to some degree in every state. This has provided a mechanism for carrying out sound land-management programs. It gives maximum responsibility to the landowners, and gives them help in developing and applying worthwhile programs. This is the only extensive natural resource management program that has developed an effective mechanism for reaching the people most directly concerned. The use of these self-governed local organizations has stimulated profound interest in broader management concepts. Many soil conservation districts have found that they cannot handle all of their problems, particularly water problems, without the cooperation of other districts in the same watershed. This realization has led to the small watershed program, which has become established legally and is now operating in most sections of the country. Many conservationists believe that the logical programs for these small watersheds can best be promoted by organizing the interrelated soil conservation districts into combined groups to work out unified programs for entire watersheds.

Unfortunately, while perhaps sound in logic, small watershed programs all too often become predominantly engineering programs that ignore other values and lack the imaginative use of techniques other than dam building, stream straightening, and drainage.

There are wide areas of agreement as to what the required natural resources policy should contain. A large group believes that we should have a joint land- and water-management policy; that the two are inseparable; and that the management of forests, grasslands, agricultural lands, wildlife, and other renewable resources is dependent upon the soundness of the plan and the thoroughness of its application to the lands and waters. This group believes that good land and water management means the management of the land in such a way as to retain as much of the rainfall as possible on that land. Many techniques have been developed for doing this, and most of them depend upon natural vegetation. This group contends that as much of the rainfall as possible should be stored in the natural reservoir of the soil and that mechanical controls, such as big dams and levees, should be constructed only to the extent needed after the more natural means of keeping the water on the land have been developed completely.

This is at direct variance with the historical concept that has prevailed for many years and that some official agencies have promoted. Concepts of water management have been built around single-purpose use, and the management projects frequently have been started with no consideration for the greatest overall use of water. Most of the original flood control structures on the Mississippi are, for example, levees and dikes on the lower river to protect cities and isolated areas from flooding. Those structures have been enlarged as the population has grown and crowded into the river valley. Now the developments have grown into gigantic and costly systems of dikes and levees that not only entail huge original investments but also continue to require tremendous annual maintenance programs to keep them reasonably effective; and, as at New Orleans in 1965, they sometimes aggravate the problems they are designed to correct.

Tasks Ahead

There is general agreement on the imperative need for a greatly expanded and accelerated program to secure hydrologic and related data. In fact, in many areas, a much greater volume of data must be obtained before an intelligent program can be formulated.

Congress in 1965 passed a Water Resources Act, which authorizes the establishment of river basin planning commissions and the making of grants to states for water-planning. Also approved was the Water Projects Recreation Act, which purports to provide a more coordinated role for fish, wildlife, and recreation project-planning. The Office of Water Resources Research in the Department of the Interior can also be construed as a move to unified planning.

All of these are steps toward a well-staffed *water resources board of review* that many believe to be a necessity.

To be completely effective, many believe that this board should be an independent unit composed of individuals not connected in any way with the agencies that propose projects.

There is general agreement that all interested govern-

mental agencies, local, state and federal, should participate and collaborate in the planning of proposed water
developments. There likewise is a strong sentiment that
citizens' groups, especially local groups of landowners,
should have a greater voice than they now have in project-
planning.

Many groups believe that a larger share of the costs
should be borne by those who benefit from such projects,
but there are different ideas as to how the costs should be
apportioned. The President's Advisory Committee on
Water Resources Policy, in its report of December, 1955,
made rather detailed recommendations covering this
aspect.

Perhaps the greatest problem in the development of
the desired natural resources policy and program is find-
ing a mechanism for making it effective. No single ac-
ceptable method has yet been proposed. Many students
of water problems doubt that it ever will be possible to
develop an effective program for coordinating the activities of the various governmental agencies that are operating in the water resources field. The Army Corps of
Engineers and the Bureau of Reclamation are huge engineering agencies, each with limited authority and restricted programs that are not always planned and
correlated for maximum resource development. In fact,
their projects often are planned with little concern for
other resources or management programs.

The President's Water Resources Policy Committee
recommended a Coordinator of Water Resources, an independent Board of Review to study economic and engineering feasibility of projects, regional or river basin
water resources committees, with a permanent Federal
Interagency Committee under the chairmanship of the

Coordinator. To be effective, both the Coordinator and the Board of Review need considerable authority if they are to deal with the official state agencies and coordinate the programs on the state level.

One of the difficulties has been the fact that, to a large extent, the federal engineering agencies have been the promoters of projects, the designers, the construction and operating agencies, and the final judges as to the desirability and feasibility of the projects. Before there can be a coordinated and intelligent approach to water- and land-management problems, it will be necessary to overcome much tradition.

Some groups believe that the soil conservation districts offer a pattern for developing coordinated programs involving both land and water. Many soil conservation districts have discovered that they cannot develop land-management programs without water management, and this fact becomes more and more apparent as their programs are applied to the land. These existing organizations, composed of those actually living on the land, accepting a considerable degree of responsibility for planning and carrying out land-management programs, offer a basis for grass-roots participation in developing coordinated land and water management that should be considered seriously.

Strengthening of many laws, as well as considerable strengthening of the soil conservation districts themselves in some states, is needed to make the program effective. Even with maximum participation by the landowners, the governmental agencies still will have an important part. The federal agencies would be obliged to continue their research activities and their role in furnishing leadership and coordination.

One basic requirement in any broad land- and water-management program is that the federal government carry out sound policies on its own lands. Congress has shown a growing tendency to recognize this responsibility, and more and more funds have been made available in recent years for the better management of federal lands. But the appropriations still are far short of the amount that is needed by the government, as a landowner, to carry its share of the load, and to furnish examples of good management.

There are many problems in connection with interstate waters, however, that undoubtedly will require participation by the federal government. Some effort has been made to handle such problems by interstate compacts, but in a number of instances these have proved to be rather slow, cumbersome mechanisms for the attainment of the objectives. Nevertheless, there is a real place for the federal government in handling major interstate water pollution problems. The states should participate much more actively in furnishing leadership and guidance in handling water and land management, and there is need for more flexible water laws in many states if the state and local projects are to provide maximum benefits. Then again, many states need to develop adequate land- and water-management programs on their lands where they, like the federal government, should demonstrate good land and water practices.

A large part of the responsibility for good land and water management rests with the private landowner. Many assume their responsibilities and have vision and imagination enough to develop and apply good management practices to their land, but such persons remain a minority. Soil conservation districts have developed local leadership among private citizens, and other groups such as forestry associations have developed commendable programs. It will be virtually impossible to get good programs undertaken by all property owners, but the adoption of a comprehensive policy would solve most of the major problems.

A coordinated effort by the federal, state, and local governments, and private landowners, is the only way in which such a program can be developed and applied. It will take a sustained educational effort over a period of many years to make such a program effective, but outstanding demonstrations have been established and can be used as guides.

One of the most pressing water-management problems is that of pollution. The vastly increased volume of municipal and industrial wastes has made good water management much more difficult. Added to this has been the increasing diffusion of long-lived agricultural pesticides, such as DDT, on land and in the waters, including the oceans. Recent legislation, both state and federal, has measurably increased the facilities and funds to deal with these wastes. Keeping pollutants out of water is becoming a laudable fixed national policy that will require great efforts to become fully effective. Air pollution in the form of chemical fumes, automobile exhaust wastes, and other by-products of industrial life is becoming a growing menace to the most necessary of all natural resources—pure air.

Many individuals, private organizations, cities, and states are concerned, and the federal government is increasingly active in seeking solutions. A policy and program in this field is needed, but progress in this direction has not been as marked as in water-pollution control.

APPENDIX A

A POLICY FOR RENEWABLE
NATURAL RESOURCES

Preamble

We, the members of the Natural Resources Council of America, in order to provide the means for a high standard of living in a healthful environment, present the following fundamental policy for the use of our basic resources of soil, water, plants, and animals, so as to maintain them through the years and prevent their waste and depletion.

To attain these objectives, we recommend the following policy:

INVENTORIES OF RENEWABLE RESOURCES

1. Adequate and continuing inventories of the renewable natural resources of the nation are needed to determine their condition, productivity, and potential use in relation to human needs and should be supported as a guide to the proper utilization and treatment of these resources.

SCIENTIFIC CONSERVATION PLAN

2. The orderly development and application of a comprehensive scientific conservation plan for every farm, ranch, small watershed, and other operating unit of the nation's land and water are imperative, and can best be achieved through the efforts of locally controlled groups.

Natural resource developments, including flood control, irrigation, and dam construction, are practically and ecologically most adequate when undertaken in relation to, or in conjunction with, upstream watershed programs.

POLICY OF USE

3. A sound policy includes the conservation, development, and proper utilization of renewable natural resources for: (a) sustained and improved agricultural production without waste, (b) protection and sustained-yield management of forest lands, (c) prevention of erosion, protection of streams from excessive siltation, and flood control to safeguard land from destructive overflow, (d) protection of community and industrial water supplies, (e) maintenance of underground water sources, (f) development and stabilization of irrigation and drainage as needed for sound land use, (g) maintenance of maximum fish and wildlife resources, (h) preservation, and proper utilization of areas best suited for needed recreational, esthetic, cultural, and ecological purposes, and (i) protection and revegetation, where necessary, of grasslands suited to range utilization.

RESPONSIBILITY OF LAND OWNERSHIP

4. Good management, public interest, and human welfare require that all landowners, public or private, care for soil and water under their control in a manner that will ensure that future generations may derive from them full enjoyment and benefit. Landowners have no moral right to abuse their lands.

PRESERVATION OF SPECIAL AREAS

5. A sufficient number of examples of every type of natural area should be preserved and kept perpetually as inviolate natural and wilderness areas for their scientific, educational,

and esthetic values. These should include examples of vegetation types and areas providing habitat for rare plants and animals. Public lands dedicated to special recreational and conservation purposes—parks, monuments, wilderness and primitive areas, wildlife refuges, and similar lands—should not be used for any purpose alien to the primary purposes of the area.

Efficient Resource Administration

6. All public service should be conducted efficiently to avoid unnecessary burden on the tax-paying public. Any overlapping functions of the several governmental agencies concerned with the administration of natural resources should be eliminated and all operations should be coordinated.

Public Participation in Conservation

7. Local, county, and state responsibility in regional and basin-wide programs, involving the use and development of soil, water, and the living resources, must include full participation in the planning, financing, management, and other phases of such programs.

National Need vs Political Expediency

8. Power developments, flood control projects, irrigation and drainage activities, and similar developments, planned and constructed largely at Federal expense, which materially change or influence existing natural resources and their protection or use, should be required to result in *national* benefit. Justification, economic and social, of projects should be realistic, should be considerate of all values, and should not rest on hopeful expectancy. Methods should be developed for equitable distribution of the project cost among the beneficiaries.

BOARD OF REVIEW

9. An independent Board of Review, composed of five members who have no affiliation with any federal agency but have outstanding interest in public affairs, should be created to review the need, cost, and desirability of all federal land and water projects and basin-wide programs. This Board should have authority to determine whether or not all projects conform to basic policies. In this way it will be possible to secure planning and consideration at every level of all phases of resource use and management, including not only hydro-electric power, flood and sediment control, navigation, irrigation, and drainage, but soil conservation, forestry, water supply, pollution abatement, recreation, fish and wildlife, parks, wilderness, and all other aspects of the entire program required for the long-range use and care of these resources.

Members of this Board should be appointed by the President to serve staggered terms and should be confirmed by the Senate. The Board should have an adequate budget and sufficient personnel to permit the prompt investigation and impartial evaluation of all development proposals. Congress should in its policy statement declare that it will not approve any proposed federal development programs nor appropriate money for such works until the findings and recommendations of this Board of Review are available.

POLICY LEGISLATION

10. To make this policy effective, Congress should pass legislation enacting it into basic law.

Adopted at the
Fifth Annual Meeting of the Council
Franklin, North Carolina, October 1, 1951

APPENDIX B

The Contributors

SHIRLEY W. ALLEN is professor emeritus of Forestry at the University of Michigan, Ann Arbor. After graduating in forestry at Iowa State College, he entered the U.S. Forest Service, rising to the position of forest supervisor. Later he served as forester for the American Forestry Association for four years. He was professor of forestry at the University of Michigan for a quarter of a century. He is a former president of the Society of American Foresters, and served as a member of the Michigan Conservation Commission. He is the author of *Introduction to American Forestry* and *Conserving Natural Resources.*

FIRMAN E. BEAR is professor emeritus of agricultural chemistry and head of the Soils Department of Rutgers University. The author of several books on soils and fertilizers, he was editor-in-chief of *Soil Science* from 1940 to 1966. He received his education at Ohio State University and the University of Wisconsin, where he received the Ph.D. degree in 1917. In 1954 Rutgers University conferred on him the honorary degree of Doctor of Science.

LOWELL BESLEY was educated in forestry at Cornell and Yale Universities. He taught forest management at the Pennsylvania State University and at West Virginia University, and was dean of the Faculty of Forestry at the University of British Columbia. During 1953–55 he was executive director and forester for the American Forestry Association. He is now chairman of the Woodlands Department, Pulp and Paper Research Institute of Canada, Montreal. He is a former chairman of the Natural Resources Council of America.

HENRY CLEPPER is a graduate of the old Pennsylvania State Forest Academy at Mont Alto. Following 15 years with the Pennsylvania Department of Forests and Waters, he served briefly in the U.S. Forest Service. During the period 1937–1965 he was executive secretary of the Society of American Foresters and managing editor of the *Journal of Forestry*. In 1966 he became associated with the Forest History Society, affiliated with Yale University at New Haven, Connecticut.

DAVID F. COSTELLO received his Ph.D. in plant ecology from the University of Chicago. After teaching botany at Marquette University for six years, he joined the U.S. Forestry Service as a research worker in range investigations. He has served as chief of the Division of Range Research at the Rocky Mountain Forest and Range Experiment Station, and also at the Pacific Northwest Forestry and Range Experiment Station, Portland, Oregon. He is the author of numerous scientific papers, bulletins, and monographs on the subject of grasslands ecology.

IRA N. GABRIELSON is president of the Wildlife Management Institute. Oregon State College conferred on him the degree of Doctor of Science and Morningside College awarded him the honorary degree of Doctor of Laws. He is a former director of the U.S. Fish and Wildlife Service, and is a recipient of the Aldo Leopold Medal awarded by the Wildlife Society. He is the author of several books, among them *Wildlife Conservation, Wildlife Management,* and *Wildlife Refuges.*

EDWARD H. GRAHAM (1907–1966) was director of the Plant Technology Division of the Soil Conservation Service until his retirement in 1964, after which he worked as a consulting ecologist. Before he joined the Department of Agriculture in 1937, Dr. Graham was for years engaged in botanical studies for the Carnegie Museum in Pittsburgh. He was author of many scientific and technical papers on plant sciences and wildlife ecology, and of several books, among them *The Land and Wildlife*, and a treatise on the application of biological principles to the management of land, *Natural Principles of Land Use*. Dr. Graham completed the revision of his chapter in this book a few weeks before his death.

ALBERT S. HAZZARD was assistant executive director of the Pennsylvania Fish Commission, Harrisburg, from 1956 until 1965 and is now engaged as a professional fishery consultant. Following receipt of his Ph.D. degree from Cornell University, he was employed as an aquatic research biologist by the U.S. Bureau of Fisheries, the Michigan Department of Conservation, and the University of Michigan. He is a former president of the American Fisheries Society.

MICHAEL NADEL, with more than two decades of conservation activity, served half of this period in New York State, including several terms as vice-president and board member of the New York State Conservation Council, and four years as a member of the advisory committee on fish and game to the New York State Conservation Commissioner. He joined the staff of The Wilderness Society in 1955. He is assistant executive director of The Wilderness Society and editor of *The Living Wilderness.*

FAIRFIELD OSBORN received his higher education at Princeton University and Cambridge University, England. He has a long career in natural resource conservation. Since 1940 he has been president of the New York Zoological Society. From 1948 to 1962, he was also president of the Conservation Foundation, New York City, and is now its Board Chairman. He is the author of *Our Plundered Planet* and *The Limits of the Earth*. He has been an officer of numerous scientific and conservation organizations in America and abroad.

JOSEPH J. SHOMON is director of the Nature Centers Division of the National Audubon Society. From 1947 to 1961 he was chief of the Division of Education of the Virginia Commission of Game and Inland Fisheries, Richmond, and editor of *Virginia Wildlife*. He is a graduate in forestry and wildlife management of the University of Michigan and received a Ph.D. degree in conservation education from that institution in 1959. Earlier in his career he was a forester with the Tennessee Valley Authority.

SELDEN LEE TINSLEY was graduated from the University of Maryland with a B.Sc. degree in agriculture and later was awarded an M.Sc. degree in forestry by the University of Idaho. His entire professional career has been with the U.S. Soil Conservation Service. He is presently serving as State Soil Conservationist for New Jersey.

WILLIAM VOIGT, JR., is executive director of the Interstate Advisory Committee on the Susequehanna River Basin at Harrisburg, Pennsylvania, and a past executive director of the Pennsylvania Fish Commission, Harrisburg. A former newspaperman, he was for ten years with the Izaak Walton League, first as national conservation director, later as executive director. He is a former chairman of the Natural Resources Council of America.

HAROLD G. WILM is assistant director of the federal Water Resources Council in Washington, D.C., having transferred in 1966 from the State University of New York, College of Forestry at Syracuse University, where he was associate dean and director of the University's Water Resources Institute. After receiving his Ph.D. degree from Cornell, he joined the U.S. Forest Service in 1932 and served in the Lake States, California, Rocky Mountain, Southern, and Pacific Northwest Forest Experiment Stations. Prior to going to Syracuse in 1953, he was chief of Watershed Research for the Forest Service. On leave from Syracuse, he served as State Conservation Commissioner in New York from 1959 until February, 1966.

HOWARD ZAHNISER (1906–1964), a well-known writer on conservation subjects, was executive director of The Wilderness Society and editor of *The Living Wilderness.* He was essayist and book editor for *Nature Magazine* for two decades, and was formerly editor and writer for the Biological Survey (now the Fish and Wildlife Service) and later head of the information division of the Bureau of Plant Industry, U.S. Department of Agriculture. He was a former chairman of the Natural Resources Council of America.

INDEX